IN RUHLEBEN
Letters from a Prisoner to His Mother

Piccadilly Circus, Ruhleben. One of the chief resorts of the camp. In the centre is the boiler-house.

[*Frontispiece.*

IN RUHLEBEN

Letters from a Prisoner to His Mother

With an account of the "University" Life, Classes, Sports, Food, Accommodation, etc., of the Internment Camp of British Prisoners :: Edited by Douglas Sladen

To which is prefixed a letter stating the case for a Wholesale Exchange of Civilian Prisoners by Sir Timothy Eden, Bart., late a prisoner at Ruhleben : :

ILLUSTRATED WITH PICTURES MADE BY STANLEY GRIMM AT RUHLEBEN AND PLANS OF THE CAMP AND DIAGRAMS OF THE BARRACKS

LONDON: HURST AND BLACKETT LTD. PATERNOSTER HOUSE, E.C. :: :: 1917

CONTENTS

PART I

PART II

LIST OF ILLUSTRATIONS

THE EDITOR'S NOTE OF ACKNOWLEDGMENT

In presenting my picture of Ruhleben I am much indebted to the Camp journal called " In Ruhleben Camp "—a cheery little periodical of 48 pages, very spiritedly illustrated. It is published sometimes monthly, sometimes fortnightly, and has, like " The Times," raised its prices as the war proceeds. It began at 2d. and is now 3d.

I believe that in the Camp some people were disappointed at its being a newspaper and not a magazine, because there was no dearth of prisoners who could have written articles worthy of the " Quarterly " or the " Cornhill."

I am thankful that they did not, for I found the reporting of the various Camp institutions and happenings among the best materials I had for visualizing Ruhleben, though at the office of one of the great London Dailies I was privileged to consult a collection of the newspaper and magazine-articles which have appeared on the subject.

I am much indebted to Sir Timothy Eden, Bart., Mr. A. D. McLaren, author of that merciless criticism of Germany entitled " Germanism from Within," just brought out by Constable and Co., Mr. Stanley Grimm, and others, lately prisoners at Ruhleben, whose names I am not at liberty to divulge.

Also to the Editors of " The Daily Mail " and " The Manchester Guardian " and " The Graphic " for permission to reproduce the plans of Ruhleben Camp which appeared in their columns.

DEDICATED TO

THE MEN WHO GRIN AND BEAR IT

AT RUHLEBEN

THE PRISONERS AT RUHLEBEN

" Travellers or residents in Germany in August, 1914," says Sir
Timothy Eden, speaking of the prisoners at Ruhleben, " they were
arrested and clapped into a concentration camp, where they have
remained ever since, ignored or forgotten by the majority of Englishmen at home."

" I have come back with a passionate longing for an interchange
of civil prisoners, where our Government can see it possible, and the
removal of the rest, who wish to go, to neutral territory."

Bishop Bury in " The Daily Telegraph."

"People who have not been there cannot realise the misery in that
camp, and should not dismiss this serious matter in a thoughtless
manner. The feeling there is—Hell could not be worse. . . . Is it
to be permitted that these conditions are to continue for a year or
two longer, at the end of which time the prisoners would return
broken in spirit and health ? "

Stanley Grimm in " The Times," November 25th, 1916.

If this book serves to recall public attention to their sufferings,
their courage and the duty of precipitating their release, it will have
served its purpose.

I ask everyone who is interested in the release of the prisoners at
Ruhleben to aid in making known to the Public and Friends the *facts*
which are given in this book.

DOUGLAS SLADEN.

TO READERS

THOSE who have not made themselves well-acquainted with the conditions of the Internment Camp of British Prisoners at Ruhleben from the articles which have been appearing in the British and American Press, and the "White Papers" of the correspondence which has been passing between the British Government and the United States Ambassador at Berlin, are recommended, before reading the letters themselves, to read the account of the circumstances of the Camp, which occupies Part II., so as to understand the allusions in the letters.

The names and initials in the letters have been changed, except where they are matters of common knowledge.

All letters from Ruhleben have to be written on notepaper with the special heading reproduced by photography with each letter in this volume.

The illustrations are by Mr. Stanley Grimm, an artist of the Expressionist School, very well-known on the Continent as an exhibitor in the *Secession Gallery* at Munich, the *Academia* at Petrograd, the *Museum* at Riga, the "*International*" at Venice, and at Dresden.

The pictures were executed at Ruhleben, where Mr. Grimm, who was exhibiting at Munich when the war broke out, was a prisoner until he was exchanged.

IN RUHLEBEN

CHAPTER I

INTRODUCTION

I

" THERE is so much studying," said Bishop Bury, speaking about the Camp at Ruhleben to a representative of "The Daily Telegraph," "that I call it the UNIVERSITY OF RUHLEBEN. There are many branches of study —music, art classes, languages, lectures on commerce, navigation, engineering and original research. There is a magnificent laboratory and classes are held in a loft with a poor light; it is a marvellous triumph over difficulties."

And to the representative of Reuter's he said: "When one thinks of the terrible conditions that prevailed during the first months of the war, and what our men with great pluck, persistence and ability have brought into existence, one cannot but have feelings of pride, thankfulness and appreciation."

In the "Letters from a Prisoner to his Mother" we can see to the fullest the workings of what I may call the CLASS-SPIRIT of Ruhleben. The writer is of the very type which has created the "University." He lives and moves and has his being in the *Classes* of the Camp School and the *Circles* of the Arts and Science Union; he studies; he lectures; he dwells with pride and affection on the work of his fellow-students and fellow-lecturers; he conducts religious services; he rejoices in his opportunities of meeting, under circumstances which lead to familiarity and friendship, with men of occupations far removed from his own (*e. g.*, we may suppose, the sailors before the mast, of whom there are many in Ruhleben), such as he would never have been likely to meet but for his captivity.

In the letters which he writes about them, to cheer and interest his mother, there is no hint of hardship, while the zest is unmistakable; they show him (without a single word about its Founder or its dogmas or its conventions) to be sustained by an earnest and unashamed Christianity, which will be welcome to many wives and parents who are yearning for their husbands and their sons in bondage at Ruhleben. In my opinion, they are as remarkable an outcome of Ruhleben as is its " University" life.

In August of last year the letters, which are so full of that " University " life, were placed in my hands by the mother to whom they were addressed. I saw at once that they were something out of the common, that they were the kind of letters which a brilliant young Oxford man of Addison's day, separated from his mother in a similar way, might have addressed to her. For they are written with a sedateness of style, for which even the nineteenth century was too breathless, and of which the twentieth century, working in shifts night and day, gives no promise.

They have more of the leisureliness and repose of the eighteenth century letters, in which style might lead to political or ecclesiastical preferment.

But it is not only a quiet and polished style which distinguishes these letters. Their high metaphysical quality and their familiarity with contemporary philosophy abroad would suggest their having been written by a philosopher, instead of an undergraduate. Yet they are the work of a twenty-year-old Oxford undergraduate, steeped in German and French philosophical and metaphysical literature as deeply as he is steeped in our own.

The style and the erudition are only the outward graces of these letters, which are equalled by the moral loftiness of their contents. For besides giving the atmosphere of the " University life " of Ruhleben, they are full of passionate filial affection, of ardent friendships and of a philanthropist's altruism, thrown into relief by the circumstances under which they have been written, since this boy is a prisoner in the Internment Camp of Ruhleben.

The very first letter he wrote from Ruhleben is taken up, not with the hardships of his surroundings, which are left unmentioned, but with their fascination.

" My life here is made very agreeable," he

says, "on account of the men whom I have had the opportunity of meeting. I do not refer to the intellectual side only. It is of intense interest to talk with men whose outlook on life is far removed from your own. On the other hand, you get to know men really well in a very short space of time."

And thereafter, in a series of letters, whose clear and carefully-chosen language is a pleasure in itself, he gives us pictures of "the gentleman as defined by the philosopher;" of the characters of his chief friends; of altruism; of friendship as defined by philosophy; of history, which he confesses that he despises; of the philosophy of work; of religion as the impetus to sacrifice; of the difference between women, who are valuable where imagination is required, and men, who are used to act within definite lines; and of philosophy's conception of woman, which is instinct with loftiness and chivalry. His appreciations of his friends are varied with appreciations of persons so opposite as Heine, with whose family he is intimate, and Joan of Arc.

The last letter is in a way an epitome of all

the rest, and culminates in one of their finest passages :

" Mother dear, there are some good friends here who have made the earth seem golden and have brought eternity into the present. But it is difficult, it is impossible to sever understanding from art. Dear H. T. and W. U. S. are two such friends. All true reward comes with original swiftness, and at times some men seem more beautiful than you could have imagined anyone being. It is at such moments that we feel the love that tried to hide itself, the tenderness that came unsought. When I think of the few things I really know, I am forced to acknowledge that they reduce themselves to the experiences of a few seemingly isolated instants when insight was granted, after love had been expended. Indeed it would not be too much to say that all that constitutes our present understanding is the sum of the love we have given in the past."

And he ends his last letter to his mother with this flash of poetry :

Introduction

" At those times when all the Earth seems clothed in the garment which Heaven only could rightly wear, you are not far away."

If his letters left any doubts of his altruism, they would be dispelled when one learns that he refused to avail himself of the order of release which had been procured for him by influential friends, on the ground that he could be of more use where he was, that he was needed by his fellows, who would feel his loss, because he was able to perform certain services for some and to make the lot of others more endurable. He is a prisoner still, when he might have been released early in the war.

Pause to think for a moment what imprisonment at Ruhleben means. I have in the latter half of this book endeavoured to convey a fair picture of it, not trying to pile up charges of brutality and what not against the Germans, but rather to show how the indomitable British spirit has met imprisonment in an unfurnished and badly victualled gaol, established in the stables of a flooded racecourse, herded at first by the non-commissioned officers of Germany.

The zeal of these N. C. O.'s was, it is true, kept within bounds by commandants who had no ill-feeling against England. But the vampire of starvation has been prowling round the lofty fences of the camp to see where it can effect an entrance, and has only been kept out by the constant stream of food sent in by faithful* friends at home and by the watchful care of the U.S. Ambassador to Germany, in administering the relief funds entrusted to him by Great Britain.

Up to this the starvation-vampire has been kept out, but the prisoners have had many other trials to contend with—miserable and over-crowded accommodation,† want of warmth, want of light, want of rooms in which to eat their food and spend their time in the hours of darkness and bad weather, want of occupation, want of news from the outside world.

* The sending of parcels has now (Jan. 1917) been standardised under strict regulations.

† As late as December 3rd, 1916, Bishop Bury pointed out in a sermon preached at St. Peter's, Vere Street, that the great evil of the place was the terrible overcrowding. He said that the overcrowding and its dangers were fully recognized by the authorities, but that when it was proposed, recently, to form another camp by taking away 700, the men petitioned to be left with the others to the end.

Introduction

I spoke just above of the indomitable British spirit. How has it been shown? I do not propose to give examples of resentment of insults which could only have one of two endings —merciless repression or merciful death, where to strike back is a physical impossibility.

Spirit can be shown as finely by the dignified refusal to let any insult ruffle your temper or degrade you in your own eyes. But neither of this do I propose to give any instances. Articles enough, which have pained the public in this direction, have been written.

What I set out to do in the picture which I have drawn of the Ruhleben Internment Camp, to explain the allusions contained in the letters, was to exhibit the zest with which these Britons threw themselves into studies and sports to solace a captivity in which, from being men of the world in full activity and freedom, they were suddenly reduced to being schoolboys and children again.

Picture an earl—who has remained incognito —a baronet, a leading Manchester solicitor and a banker—to take no further instances— finding themselves with only ten shillings a week to spend ; sent to bed at a quarter to nine in the winter and a quarter to ten in the summer ; (at first) under the absolute control of common guards ; fed at a seven-thirty breakfast on dry bread and acorn coffee, at a twelve-noon dinner with soup made of water bewitched, vegetables begrudged and meat forgotten, and at a half-past five supper given no more than poor and watery tea or acorn coffee, with the same accompaniment of dry bread.

Picture them sleeping six in a horse-box, or a hundred in a loft, in which they could not turn on their bed-sacks without waking a neighbour. Picture them having to take a long walk in the cold and wet to wash themselves—and for the matter of that, their clothes also—in an open shed. Picture them drying their washing and eating their food in their horse-boxes and stable-lofts, with scanty daylight by day and only the glimmer, from a passage, of artificial light by night. Picture them having to go, bowl in hand, for their meals, like paupers at a soup-kitchen, to distant kitchens where it took two hours to distribute the phantom meal to the weary prisoners standing in queues.

Introduction

And then picture the four thousand, mostly nurtured with the comforts of the British middle class (in spite of these hardships, beside which the men suffering penal servitude in British prisons are as pigs in clover), keeping up a good heart and going about their business of study and sport as cheerily as boys who have merely exchanged the sybarisms of home for the spartanisms of a public-school.

It is magnificent. And in spite of all their hardships and restrictions, they are reaping the reward of it already, for instead of losing his reason from monotony and want of hope, the man who determines to keep his eye and his hand true and his body vigorous with the sports of his country, and to use his enforced leisure to be an altogether better-educated man when his long captivity is over, remains, if he is sufficiently nourished, as fit as a public-school boy —that type of the race, though his mind *must*, if only unconsciously, feel the strain.

It is proper to point out that the prisoners have only been kept in vigour because friends at home have sent them a steady supply of food-parcels, and because, thanks to the British Government, those who had no money themselves have received their weekly dole like the rest. But everyone has had to share with less fortunate neighbours, and it has been mighty plain living which has gone with the high thinking of Ruhleben.

These are the surroundings and the circumstances in which that Oxford undergraduate wrote those remarkable letters.

In this context I must refer to the work of the representatives of the United States on behalf of the prisoners at Ruhleben and elsewhere. To the achievements of the U.S. Ambassador at Berlin and his staff, especially Mr. G. W. Minot and Dr. A. E. Taylor, to their constant supervision, to their exposure of abuses, to their championship of the helpless, to their immense labours in administration, constant reference is made in this book.

But there are others, like Mr. Morgan, the United States' Consul-General at Hamburg, who have done equally sterling work, though it has only occasionally come into these pages.

Mr. Morgan's work lay in helping innocent fugitives to leave the country by hook or by crook—that is, by influence with the German authorities or by ingenuity—and in doing all he could to alleviate the misfortunes and hardships of those for whom he could procure no exit. He was like a father to the fugitives with whom Hamburg was for two reasons crowded —because it was a natural exit from Germany and because it had larger connections with England than any other place in Germany. The streets round the Consulate were black with thousands of people, and he worked morning, noon and night to get them all off. He saw many of them off personally, one after another.

In conclusion, I ask myself what the late W. P. Frith, R.A., that wonderful cinematographer of a day's events on a single gigantic canvas, would have put into his picture if he had been asked to paint a companion-picture to his famous " Derby Day " of the Internment Camp at Ruhleben ?

Item : Twenty-three great barracks, some evolved out of stables, some built for prison-dormitories.

Item : A grand-stand, with its rising tiers turned into open-air class-rooms.

Item: Half the core of a racecourse, with goal-posts or cricket-stumps, golf-green-flags, tennis-nets and other hubs of British sport, rising out of the turf.

Item: Four thousand British men, surprisingly British in their appearance, in spite of the makeshifts of poverty; some of them engaged in a desperate rivalry of sport, which for the time takes away the knowledge of Good and Evil that Eve gathered from the fatal tree; some of them, too old or too unsuited for sport, engaged in eternal walks and talks, which lead nowhere, but are conducted with the cheeriness which combats the idea of being down-hearted; and some of them, both old and young, doing the Englishman's grouse, with more excuse than usual.

Item: The pipes and the cigarettes in the mouths of the golfers and those engaged in other sports not too strenuous, and all the walkers and talkers who are not non-smokers or "stony-broke."

These walkers and talkers, the players such as are not too strenuously engaged in sport for the everyday man in them to be showing—how would

Bird's-eye view of the Racecourse at Ruhleben, showing on the left the Grand Stand in which the classes and entertainments were held, and on the right the barracks in which the prisoners lived.

he have to depict them? Not a high per-
centage (except merchants in business in Germany) as important, wealthy or middle-aged
people—and these, such as they were, chiefly
taking cures when the evil day broke; a certain
number of persons who have been studying
music and art; the first rush of summer holiday-
makers, among whom Mr. Hughes saw most
conspicuously undergraduates, Public-School
masters and invalids for the spas; most of
the golf professionals of Germany; a few
unclaimed jockeys and trainers; but above
all, the seamen and ships' stewards from the
British ships which were in German harbours
when the war started; foremen and workmen
who were teaching German factories how to
capture British trade—small luck to them;
and—perhaps more numerous than any—teachers
of English resident in Germany, whether attached
to universities or in private practice; stray
individuals in many strange trades, from
millionaire's coachman to Canadian trapper.

Would he not have added the naturalized,
full-blooded Germans, who used their naturali-
zation to escape serving in the German Army

and blackguarded England because they were punished for so doing, and the " crowd of Englishmen who did not speak English at all, but used to give lessons in their own lingo in return for instruction in their mother-tongue ? "

If he had painted his great Ruhleben picture to depict indoor life, what then ?

Item : Classes innumerable ! Teachers—a hundred or more—taking advantage of every bit of cover from the elements ; rooms cold and few ; light almost too dim for reading.

Item : A grand hall, built under a grand-stand, like a cupboard under a stair, divided into a cinema and a hall for general entertain-ments. In the latter, drama four times a week, Divine services, debates, lectures, committee-meetings and concerts.

Item : Prisoners' stores, of the Army and Navy or Civil Service Supply Association pattern, and petty shops—barbers', mending-tailors', cobblers', shoeblacks and the like, dotted about in the corners of buildings.

Item : A post-office for prisoners' parcels, a thousand of them in a day sometimes.

Item : A police-station, little more than a lost-property-office.

While for his background, he would have had :

Item : The three grand-stands and the running-track, to remind you that Ruhleben was in inception a fashionable racecourse.

Item : The lofty walls and fences, topped with barbed wire, to remind you that it is a prison in being. ,

II

Into the questions of rival committees, of the Captains withholding from the Camp the accounts of the money earned by the prisoners' entertainments, and other matters of what I may call camp-politics, I have not entered much, though they agitated the Camp sufficiently to call for the notice of the American Ambassador.

Nor have I myself entered into the more acute questions between the British and German Governments with relation to the comparative treatment of prisoners in the two countries and proposed measures for exchange, because, for one thing, I did not wish to plunge into any contentious matter without greater personal knowledge, and because, for another, the letters on which my chapters are a commentary are very aloof from such matters ; and above all, because I personally hold such strong views upon the matter, that I wished to leave it severely alone. The food conditions at Ruhleben, for instance, appear to me to be worse than those at Wittenberg, so uncompromisingly described in "The Story of a Prisoner of War."

Fortunately there is no need for me to express my views when Sir Timothy Eden, in his admirable letter to "The Times," which I reprint with his permission, has stated the whole case so convincingly. He is exactly the right man to have done it, because not only has he lately been released from Ruhleben himself, but his name is one which carries weight in America as well as England, since he is the direct descendant and heir of the founder of the State of Maryland.

I have said that the case could not have been better put than it has been by Sir Timothy. The luridness of the picture which he draws throws into all the greater prominence the character of these letters, the splendid pluck with which the British interned in Ruhleben contrive, in spite of the poverty and the primitive conditions in which they are kept, to maintain their sports and classes.

In the " Letters from a Prisoner to his Mother " there is not one word which indicates the hardships which the writer was enduring.

They are written as if there was no such thing as a hardship, hardly any such thing as captivity, the obvious intentions of the writer being to banish all anxiety from his mother's heart and to apply the lessons of philosophy, the study of which he had found so enthralling, to their legitimate use, of making him who had learned them think it :

> " . . . . . nobler in the mind to suffer
> The slings and arrows of outrageous fortune. . . ."
> *Hamlet* iii. 1

DOUGLAS SLADEN.

The Avenue House,
  Richmond, Surrey.
    January 15*th*, 1917.

THE PRISONER AT RUHLEBEN

" To-day, beneath the foeman's frown,
    He stands in Elgin's place,
Ambassador from Britain's crown,
    And type of all her race.

*   *   *   *   *

" He only knows, that not through *him*
    Shall England come to shame."
             " The Private of the Buffs."
                 Sir Francis Hastings Doyle.

[*Photo by F. A. Swaine.*

SIR TIMOTHY EDEN, BART.

[*Facing p. 20.*

CHAPTER II*

CIVILIAN PRISONERS:

THE CASE FOR A WHOLESALE EXCHANGE

BY

SIR TIMOTHY EDEN, BART.

NOW that we are faced with another winter the thoughts of many are naturally turned to the soldiers in the trenches—and, equally naturally perhaps, comparatively few people are thinking of the prisoners in Germany ; for out of sight is too often out of mind. There are two classes of prisoners—military and civilian. The former are much to be pitied, but at the same time we must realize that theirs is a recognized position. They have been fighting against a nation, they have been taken by that nation,

* Written in the form of a letter to " The Times " of Nov. 22 1916, and published in full by his permission.

and the inevitable result is internment. Every
man who goes to the front fully realizes that he
may be made prisoner, and if he be so, at least
he has had a run for his money. All we can do
here is to try to alleviate the hardships of his
captivity. But there are a few thousand Englishmen in Germany, who are dignified by the title
of *civilian* prisoners of *war*—the very expression
being a contradiction in terms. These have
no recognized position, but have been the
constant cause of bickerings and arguments
since the beginning of the war. Travellers or
residents in Germany, in August, 1914, they
were arrested and clapped into a concentration
camp, where they have remained ever since,
ignored or forgotten by the majority of Englishmen at home. They have had no run for their
money. I will not dwell upon their physical
sufferings. They have been many, but no worse
than, and in many cases not so bad as, those of
countless other sufferers in this war, but I cannot
lay too much stress upon the serious mental
condition of the civilian prisoners. And this
condition is only natural. Suddenly snatched
from their peaceful occupations, these men have

been herded into a racecourse, where they have now lived in crowded stables for two years. For not one single instant during the whole of that time has any prisoner had the slightest privacy.

It is impossible to be alone. There are no past glories to dream about. No consolation in the remembrance of duty done. The men have nothing to think of save their ruined prospects and the hopelessness of their position. Therefore, I say again that the mental state of these prisoners is most serious. And it is imperative if they are to retain their reason that they should be set free at once. As I, myself, have been comparatively recently released from Ruhleben I can speak with authority. Now, it seems that at last all civilians over forty-five are to be exchanged. This is good news. But it comes after two years of waiting which have claimed a heavy toll. Why could it not have been done at once? And are the others to wait another two years till they too are released? If so, the state of these men when they reach England will be pitiful indeed. Is it to be wondered at if the prisoners in Ruhleben murmur against the slow

23

and comfortable deliberations of the authorities at home, and complain that they are being neglected by their countrymen? There is only one way of obtaining the release of the British civilians. We must give Germany all her civilians in exchange. That is to say that we must give 26,000 and receive 4,000. The disadvantages of such a step are obvious. But, granted that Germany will gain 20,000 more fighting men, what is this number compared to the millions that are now engaged in the war? The effect that 20,000 men can produce on a battlefield of nations must be so small as to be imperceptible. Such a number would be a mere drop in the ocean. Again, when these German prisoners arrive in their homes, and compare the state of affairs in their country to life in England, will they not produce a bad impression and even discontent and mistrust? And what will happen to these Germans if they are kept here till the war is over? They will quietly settle down once more to their businesses. Is this to be desired? Finally, if this exchange be effected, Germany will have 26,000 men to feed well, instead of 4,000 indifferently, and we, on the other hand, will be saved much expense. Therefore, from several points of view we should not lose entirely by carrying out this scheme. But even were we to lose and lose again, it would yet be our bounden duty to insist on the release of all British civilians.

These must now face another Berlin winter on an open racecourse, and if they are to be left for the third time during the cold months without any prospect of deliverance, they will suffer more terribly than we can imagine.* Unless they are released—not at some dim future date, but at once—the burden of responsibility to their wives and families will be a heavy one to bear, and that responsibility will fall upon their fellow-countrymen.

* Mr. F. W. Hanson writes to " The Times," January 11, 1916 :

"The men at Ruhleben still live in stables, stable lofts, and wooden huts, all of which are terribly overcrowded, though not quite as badly as they were in the early days of the Camp. They still have to live day and night in the same quarters—that is, they sleep, live and eat in the same miserable bit of space allotted to them by the German authorities. . . . . They are still compelled to live upon their own parcels sent to them from home, and the food provided for the Camp by the Germans is still so poor and so insufficient that they would die of starvation if their flow of parcels should cease. I have seen men so die n the early days of the camps before the parcels' service was organized."

CHAPTER III

JUST as this book was about to go to the printer, Bishop Bury returned—(according to the papers it was on December 2nd)—from a visit to the Internment Camp at Ruhleben, to see the circumstances under which our men have begun their third winter there.

Since he is Bishop of North and Central Europe, he is the Diocesan of the prisoners—and incidentally of Germany—and therefore enjoyed greater privacy in his dealings with them than the German Government would have accorded to any other Englishman. He is, I believe, the only Englishman who has been allowed into Germany since the beginning of the war. He brings, also, much later information of the camp than has come from any other source, even letters, the last of which to be received before this book went to press, were dated October 26th.

In this chapter I depend entirely on what I have read in Reuter's interview with him and the interviews and reports of his visit to Ruhleben which I have read in the various newspapers. I propose to consider certain of his statements in the light of what we have heard from Sir Timothy Eden and Mr. A. D. McLaren, both of whom have themselves been prisoners in the Internment Camp at Ruhleben. The Bishop is the only optimist of the three, and he performed his difficult task of being honest about the prisoners, while he evinced his gratitude to the German Government, very tactfully.

To me it seems that the German authorities treated him unimaginably well, for they gave him free permission to tell the prisoners of the progress of the war from the English point of view, and they permitted the prisoners to sing "God Save the King" (twice, at his request), besides allowing him to take uncensored messages and letters to their friends ; and, as he informed his congregation at St. Peter's, Vere Street, in the first sermon which he preached after his return, " when I visited the War Office at Berlin, I was not only assured of sympathy, but was positively charged by those in authority to do everything to hearten up our men, everything to appeal to their patriotism."

Permission was given him, he said to " The Evening Standard " representative, because he was known in Germany in his episcopal capacity in time of peace—and, in fact, it came through the good offices of the Oberbürgermeister of Munich, who had been a real friend to the English Church, although a Roman Catholic. The Oberbürgermeister appealed to Berlin, and was so influential that at last his wish was acquiesced in by the authorities.

And we learn from " The Daily Mail " that a young Berlin judge, with a Captain's rank, was sent to meet him at the Swiss frontier and escort him directly to Ruhleben. There he was assigned a room in the administrative quarters, with an orderly, who slept in an adjoining room, to do his bidding, and he was invited to mingle with the prisoners at will, without any sort of interference from the German officers or guards.

Accordingly, though possibly he had his midday meal (which is not mentioned) at the Casino, where certain privileged (and chiefly invalid) prisoners are allowed to buy their food, he had breakfast, tea and supper with the prisoners, in their various horse-boxes and lofts, specially mentioning a party of old Etonians, a party of prisoners from Hamburg and a party of prisoners from Frankfurt.

He was present at an Association football match, at which he kicked off, at a play in the theatre under the Grand Stand, and at special concerts which were arranged for him; he held four services on Sunday; he spent his spare moments in receiving those uncensored messages and letters from the prisoners to their friends in England, each prisoner being limited to a three-minutes' interview. The Bishop asked the German authorities if he might live in the Camp, because otherwise, the prisoners, who are very patriotic, might not have had confidence in him. He spent his whole time with them, except when he visited the German War

Office at Berlin and the British Officers' Camp at Blankenberg.

To Reuter's representative he said, " This never-to-be-forgotten week among my countrymen has made me more thankful than ever that I am an Englishman, and if I am not very much mistaken my imprisoned countrymen at Ruhleben have made the enemy respect us and our brave men at the Front."

*   *   *   *   *

" The Camp Censor—a German officer—is an absolutely fair and straight man, in full sympathy with the prisoners.* Although he could have done so, had he wished, he never once attended a meeting at which I spoke, and I was allowed to bring away every note I made and every paper given to me. In fact, I was never once prevented in the slightest degree from full and uninterrupted connection with the men from start to finish. On the last night of my stay I obtained permission for the prisoners to sing ' God Save the King,' and this was

* There are many corroborations of this in the letters.

An episode in the game.

[*Facing p.* 30.

repeated when I addressed the whole Camp in the open air. I shall never forget the scene of indescribable enthusiasm."

*　　*　　*　　*　　*

" I may add that all letters from the men may be relied upon as accurate, as practically all those with whom I came in contact said that they found it so difficult to persuade relations at home that they were not keeping something back."

Here the Bishop is in direct conflict with Mr. McLaren,* who says that if a prisoner dared to mention that he was even ill in a letter, the letter was destroyed by the authorities.

But the Bishop did not mince words at all to Mr. Frederick William Wile, who, as the representative of " The Daily Mail," saw him on his return :

" ' The bitter end,' the Bishop said, ' would speedily come, I fear, for many of our fellows except for parcels from home. *I wish to say that parcels are absolutely vitally necessary to the existence of the men at Ruhleben.* They would

* Author of " Germanism from Within."

starve or freeze to death without them. For both food and clothing they are dependent upon us. They cannot eat the rations provided by the German authorities. The rations may be digestible to Germans, but Britons who are not used to them simply cannot stomach them. Thanks to an organization for which, as for so many things, we are indebted to our American official friends in Berlin, every prisoner at Ruhleben is now assured of a parcel.* But any cessation of the supply—any interference by the German authorities, for example—would certainly be fraught with grave peril to our men. *We must keep up the parcels at all costs.'* "

On the same subject, he made a statement to " The Daily Telegraph " representative which appears to me perfectly incredible—in fact, I thought it was a misprint, but see that other papers have given the same figures.

" ' The morning before I came away, 80,000 parcels arrived from home. The day previous to that there were 56,000.' "

In another interview he gives the number of

* See next page.

prisoners as 3,600; 3,600 into 136,000 works out at 38 parcels apiece in two days. But since, according to the American Ambassador's Report, there are practically 750 prisoners who receive no parcels from friends, there must have been an average of 48 parcels apiece in two days for the more fortunate prisoners.

Supposing that a nought had crept in, and that the figures should have been 8,000 and 5,600, that would have been sufficiently remarkable, since in October, 1915, the average number of parcels to arrive in a day was 1,000 and the greatest number recorded 1,600.

Even allowing that these were the Christmas parcels sent a month in advance, to escape the 15th-to-25th-of-December moratorium of the German Government, it would be difficult, I think, to find one mortal sufficiently generous to send an imprisoned relative about fifty parcels, let alone 2,850 donors equally generous. I do not say that it is not a fact, but if it is, it is beyond my capacity to understand.

The Bishop is certainly commendably outspoken. He told Mr. Wile:

" ' At best it was easy to observe that two

years of strain and restraint are beginning to tell on the strongest of the prisoners. I could see that from the ease with which tears would often rush to their eyes when I was in personal contact with them. The younger fellows, naturally, bear up best, but sooner or later they, too, yield to the nerve-pressure which has already broken middle-aged and older men. Except for these nerve-cases there is practically no sickness of consequence at Ruhleben. At Dr. Weiler's Sanatorium in West End* I saw sixty or seventy nerve-cases, all due to the soul-wrecking regime of the Camp. I gathered that Dr. Weiler's patients are now well-treated.

" ' Our men confess that their toughest fight is against collapse of mind and spirit. I am proud, as an Englishman, to report that thus far they are waging a successful fight. Twenty-four months are enough to accustom almost any man even to existence in over-crowded horse-boxes and barracks indifferently ventilated and badly illuminated.' "

This statement of the Bishop's tallies exactly

* Mr. Grimm, who was at Dr. Weiler's Sanatorium, says that the food was very insufficient in quantity. See page 197.

with what Sir Timothy Eden and Mr. Stanley Grimm have said above.

One can understand that the men who justly filled the Bishop with such admiration for what he calls " the University of Ruhleben "— meaning the wonderful system of classes and circles for study which they have established —and the men who carry out their love of sports in the " cabined, cribbed, confined " fields of Ruhleben, as they would on cricket, football, golf and tennis grounds at home, feel the oppression less than those who are physically unfit or prefer moping to study. But the element of physical hardship must tell upon all, except those who have been accustomed to it from childhood, and they are not numerous at Ruhleben, with the exception of sailors, who for another reason might feel the confinement.

The Bishop clearly supports Sir Timothy Eden's contention that something should be done at once to procure the transfer of Ruhleben prisoners to Switzerland, if their release cannot be effected. How this is to be done, I leave to Sir Timothy to argue (on page 24).

If this book is devoted not to dwelling on the prisoners' " deteriorating and embittering conditions," but to what (in the Bishop's words to " The Daily Telegraph ") " British character, grit and determination, with the aid of people at home, have made of this Camp," it is not because I see the necessity for their release any less than the Bishop, or Sir Timothy, or Mr. Grimm, but because I believe that the British Public—and, I hope, the British Parliament—will be moved on their behalf by their pluck as well as by their sufferings.

I have given due space to the sports and entertainments with which they keep up their health and their courage, but the real subject of the book is what the Bishop calls " The University of Ruhleben," for the " Letters from a Prisoner to his Mother," which give it its name and form its backbone, present to us in an extraordinary degree the atmosphere of " the University."

CHAPTER IV

CONCERNING THE AUTHOR OF THE LETTERS

THE writer of these letters, whom we will call " Richard Roe," is an Oxford undergraduate. When the long summer vacation of 1914 came, he met his mother at Hamburg, and they were going on to Switzerland together. But the war broke out, and it was impossible for him to leave, though no one in Hamburg would believe that England would join in the war.

The day before England declared war, " Mrs. Roe " went with her son to the British Consulate in Hamburg to see that his passport was all right. There was an enormous crowd there, but the Consul saw her, shook hands with her and said, " Come to-morrow morning, and we will arrange the whole thing then."

She and her son then went off, but when they

got back to the Consulate on the next morning, they found a large placard outside it, stating that the British Consul and his whole staff had left during the night and that all the British in

Englánderlager Ruhleben   Kriegsgefangenensendung

Mrs. Margaret Roe.

London

S. W.

Absender *Richard Roe.*

Baracke *13*

Box *16*   Datum *15 March 1915*

Official Envelope of the Internment Camp at Ruhleben.

Hamburg must go to the American Consul and be provided with fresh passports, as their British ones were of no more value.

Richard Roe had arrived in Hamburg the day before Germany mobilized, and when he found how things were, had wanted to get away, but it was impossible, owing to the fact that all the trains which were running in the direction of Flushing, and westwards generally, were being used for the German Army and no civilians were allowed on them. His mother went straight to the British Consul, who, the first

Official Postcard of the Internment Camp at Ruhleben.

time she went to him, said, " Oh, just wait for a few days—then things will have all settled down."

The boy had been several times in Germany before, and spoke German and French as perfectly as he spoke English.

He was in the Officers' Training Corps at

school, and was good at sports, having taken prizes for gymnastics, swimming, diving and boxing.

He had before the war no definite sympathy with either of the political parties in England. He was an omnivorous reader. Among the authors he studied most were Browning, Gilbert Murray, Walter Pater, Lowes Dickinson, Plato, Kant, Fichter, Schopenhauer, Nietzsche, Eutken, Bergson, and philosophers generally, from Marcus Aurelius to Mr. Balfour. He was a great reader of Goethe.

When he went to Oxford first, he formed a little circle, where they used to lecture to each other. The subject on which he chose to lecture was the Scandinavian novelist, Strindberg. He knows whole passages of Walter Pater's writings by heart.

While he was at school and Oxford, in order to stimulate his interest in the study of the philosophers, his mother, who is a fine linguist, always read the same books as he did, and they discussed them in their correspondence.

Undoubtedly, it is due to his having such a mother that we owe the quality of these letters.

RACE COURSE

ROAD

[Reproduced by permission from "The Manchester Guardian."]

Ground plan of the Camp at Ruhleben in which the prisoners were interned.

" To those whose love continues, even the dead may turn and bow, and though the rose might marvel at the sweetness of the breeze, she would not quench the perfume she exhaled."

From the letter of June 21, 1916.

PART I

CHAPTER V

* Jungfrauen Tal,
Hamburg,
28th January, 1915.

MY DARLING MOTHER,

To write you an expression of my
feelings of gratitude and affection towards you
is useless, since in the relationship between
personalities it makes no difference what you
say, and very little difference what you do,
while all depends simply and solely on what
you *are*. Frequently I have heard it said, but
never with greater beauty and feeling than in
a sermon at Oxford by Mr. T. R. Glover of

* The first letter, included, although it was not written at
Ruhleben, makes an appropriate beginning.

43

Cambridge, that whatever outward coolness they might observe, those, at any rate, who had children were often painfully conscious of the fact that they were known extremely well. The reverse side of the same coin is true in my case, for I, who have a mother, know how piercingly accurate is the knowledge which you have of me. But as for my knowledge of you, dear mother, it is like life itself, gaining its value from being indeterminably deep, so that any advance on my part merely means a greater recognition of the impossibility of ever reaching the end. The reason for this is clear to every sympathetic eye. We have never consciously tried to understand each other. You will have met many people in your life who presented to you a purely intellectual problem, which lost its interest when it had been solved. You had then " understood " them and dismissed them. But between sympathetic relationships such as that between us two, *there never exists a problem*, and as a result not the intellect but the heart is applied, and, while a vastly greater depth is reached, an *unfathomable* depth is opened out.

Life as far as it lies behind me has brought

me into touch with many changing aspects, yet there is but one which I would wish to tell you now—namely, that the small share I was able to have as a praepostor in raising the moral tone in my house at school, was in no small measure due to the kindly influence which radiated from you. Other things of more apparent interest I might mention, but let this be a sample to you of what I value highest in life.

At the present, though for my part I do not for a moment budge from my own position, the aspect of the war as I have seen it here, and which saddens me beyond measure, is the tragedy of the fight between men, each of whom goes out to champion "the right," and each of whom has before him his ideals, and the example of what is greatest in all that he knows. It was with such thoughts in my mind that I wrote the little composition last Sunday, which I sent you.

Some day we shall all have perfect knowledge and perfect understanding of pure truth. Where we have failed, such absolute knowledge of the entire extent and influence of our faults will in itself actually be the punishment, while where we have done our best, pure vision shall be the highest reward. Above all, there shall be forgiveness. But that is not yet and not here.

I would tell you finally, mother dear, that my main feeling, apart from the reflective mood in which I wrote some of the lines, and apart from my sorrow at leaving *you* and my anxiety about *you*, my main feeling—that is, above my own personal future—is the curiosity of the interested spectator. I am, as far as exterior treatment goes, merely a name on a document, so that I really start looking upon my body as simply one of the things belonging to me.

Within, however, the embers are glowing with pride in you and love for you, and the determination to progress in such a manner that you shall never feel ashamed of me.

When you write to F. U—n give him my heartfelt love.

Your ever loving son,
RICHARD.

Absender:

Richard Roe.

~~Taglan Gerlager Ruhleben~~

Baracke *13*

Box *16*

15th March, 1915.

An -To Mrs *Margaret Roe* On *London. S.W.*

be -Straße No.

GELD IST AN INTERNIERTE PERSÖNLICH ZU SENDEN
UND ZWAR AUSSCHLIESSLICH DURCH POSTANWEISUNG
- AUF DER RÜCKSEITE DES ABSCHNITTES IST DER
VOLLE NAME DES EMPFÄNGERS ZU WIEDERHOLEN

MONEY TO BE SENT BY POSTAL ORDER
ONLY NOT PER REGISTERED LETTER -
ADDRESSEE'S FULL NAME MUST BE WRIT-
TEN LEGIBLY ON COUNTERFOIL SLIP

DARLING MOTHER,

Many, many thanks for all your parcels
and communications. Your letters cheered me
up very greatly, and the contents of the parcels
refreshed the inner man; so that all is well
with me in body and mind. The books arrived
with incredible speed, and I was overjoyed to
receive them. Particularly am I grateful to
Mrs. K. for lending me the volume of Keller,*
of which I am taking great care. Keller is just
the right author for this camp, and the more
intimately you enter into his mind, the more
like a real friend does he become. You see his
faults, but they are the faults of a friend, and

* Gottfried Keller, the great Swiss novelist, born near Zurich,
1819; died 1890.

while you do not pardon them, you hardly wish them gone.

Please convey my very kindest regards to the K.'s. I have read " Der Grüne Heinrich " with great pleasure. At the end of the week I am giving a little lecture on Keller to a circle of friends, though for a serious study of the man the books of reference are lacking. Perhaps this is a good thing, for ordinarily you accustom yourself too much to books of reference and books about books.

I am quite touched to hear that some dear people have actually thought of me. Please give the old lady my hearty thanks. Mrs. H. also has written me a card herself, and expressed herself charmingly. But then, you see, she is Mrs. H. I need say no more. F. V. sends you and her his very best regards. We have frequently talked of those teas at her place, set among beautiful surroundings, and suffused with all the charm of a dilettanti literary conversation.

My life here is made very agreeable on account of the men I have had the opportunity of meeting. I do not refer to the intellectual side only. It is of intense interest to talk with men whose outlook on life is far removed from your own. On the other hand, you get to know men really well in a very short space of time. In the afternoons I usually work with a college friend of mine, who is studying the same subject as I am. Altogether, I must say that I have met some of the finest men here that it has ever been my good fortune to converse with.

But I must answer some of your questions. I have not paid Frau N. for February. She was always paid at the end of the month. Please do not send me any more margarine. The pen works well, but F. V. is quite satisfied with his, and so does not need any more. The pork cutlets in tins you sent were brilliant, and are well worth sending. They are the best tinned meat F. V. has had here, and we made a lunch-party from them, one of the toasts being: " To our absent friends in England and on the Continent."

I have had two cards from Mr. U—n, and have communicated with him about money. The fact is that I want very little money.

Mother, dear, I am afraid that I am giving you an excessive amount of trouble ; but please send me Bergson : " Introduction to Meta-physics," a little blue book on the second shelf from the top—at least, I think it is there. Could you also send F. G. and me two writing-blocks each with large pages ?

I am very pleased indeed that Mr. I. has had leave to go and hope to hear from you when he has arrived safely. Please give my kindest regards to Mrs. H. I am very sorry that N. H. has been ill.

This letter may be delayed, but I hope that you will not be over-anxious about me, particu-larly since I am in such good health, owing to the parcels and care. I do not know how to thank you for the care you have been taking with the parcels, and I am in a position to appreciate what an amount of trouble they require. Please give my love to the J.'s. Their boys are in good health. You are frequently in my mind, but I like to think of you as bright and as confident as your loving

RICHARD.

Absender:

Richard Roe.

Engländerlager Ruhleben

Baracke *13*

Box *16*

14th *April*, 1915.

An -To Mrs *Margaret Roe* On *London. S.W.*

-Straße No.

GELD IST AN INTERNIERTE **PERSÖNLICH** ZU SENDEN
UND ZWAR AUSSCHLIESSLICH DURCH POSTANWEISUNG
- AUF DER RÜCKSEITE DES ABSCHNITTES IST DER
VOLLE NAME DES EMPFÄNGERS ZU WIEDERHOLEN

MONEY TO BE SENT BY POSTAL ORDER
ONLY NOT PER REGISTERED LETTER -
ADDRESSEE'S FULL NAME MUST BE WRIT-
TEN LEGIBLY ON COUNTERFOIL SLIP

DARLING MOTHER,

Many thanks for your parcels, letters and cards. The former were evidently selected with great care, and the latter seemed like chats with you. The Easter eggs were delicious, and on arrival of the Easter parcels we had a most enjoyable lunch together. Please thank that Dutch lady very much for sending those Easter eggs. It was charming of her to remember me. Your selection has been excellent each time. I cannot thank you in detail. Don't trouble to send me any more tins of vegetables ; we get plenty. F. G. does not want any more stores for the present, but a steak, for instance, as you mention, is always welcome as a change. The tinned meat is very good.

In Ruhleben

I don't believe I ever told you how my lecture on Keller went off. It seems like ancient history by now. My friends were pleased, but I was not. It was all right as far as it went, but I had made too many notes and got too much that I wanted to work out. I only succeeded in explaining what I had meant to be the first part. I gave them the outlines of his life and literary productiveness, then I ran through three of his most marked traits—lack of self-consciousness, sincerity and the organic view—and found in almost every example that I gave that Goethe served admirably as a comparison or contrast, as the case might be. Contrast, for instance, Goethe's discussion of the French drama in " Dichtung und Wahrheit," supposed to have been held at the age of twelve, and Keller's experience of amateur theatricals at the same age. One of my hearers has since then bought " Die Leute von Seldwyla," and several have read parts. Once four of us read " Romeo und Juliet " together. At present I. has the book.

Our box is delightfully grouped, since C. came into it nearly four weeks ago. He is a most able fellow, and we have most interesting times together. His friends also are fine, keen young men. It sounds selfish to talk about myself the whole time, but I know it is that which will interest you chiefly.

For the last three weeks I have been taking an intermediate French class. The school is not yet going in full swing, but is starting gradually. Larger classes will be taken in the open air, as the weather gets warmer. My present class consists of six members. Their standard differs considerably, and their personalities, from that of a sailor to that of a graduate of Aberdeen University. Besides this, I have been helping a couple of fellows with some elementary Latin, and shall take one of them in Greek also.

I am also reading Schiller's plays with Q. and some others. As regards my own work, I am at present working through the Theaetetus of Plato.

You see, there is no lack of interest, but a good deal of it is a mere attempt to fill in the time with a minimum of loss to others and oneself. The only, or almost the only, work of value is, of course, the quiet work you do by yourself, while the men with whom you come into contact must necessarily be of more vital interest than reading. Much of the interest here is, of course, contained in the extraordinary situations in which men are found. It is not everywhere that a respectable business man on the shady side of thirty-five is tickled as he gets into bed. Of little humorous incidents there are plenty, but the serious side is there, in all conscience.

Last Wednesday evening was the first time I took a public religious service. There is a service every Wednesday evening. Since Friday last a few of us have got a little room in which we take it in turns to read service in the morning.

Sport, also, is being organized, and Rugby football has started, as well as regular Association. On Easter Monday I played in the first Rugger exhibition match—the Universities and Public Schools against the Merchant Service.

You can send me a whole case of Nestlé's milk. Members of my box tell me that they will gladly take part of the consignment. Send whatever you don't want yourself. Also send me from the grocer's on the Gänsemarkt by the *Lessing Theater* some Grape-nuts, if he still has them, otherwise a packet of *Weizenflocken.** Also " The Disciple," by Paul Bourget, Nelson Edition, one Mark. Boysen probably has it. Also, if you can find them without trouble among my books: Sonnenschein's Greek Grammar, Chardenal's French Exercises (a little red book at the bottom), Cicero, any two volumes of edited speeches.

I am so sorry to give you all this trouble. Don't bother to look for the Chardenal if you don't find it quickly.

My kindest regards to Mr. H. C. also sends you and him his regards. Please remember me to all the kind people, especially Mrs. H.

Much love and kindly thoughts from your
RICHARD.

---

* Shredded Wheat.

Absender:

Richard Roe.

Engländerlager Ruhleben

Baracke *13.*

Box *16.*

18*th May*, 1915.

An – To M*rs* *Margaret Roe* On *London. S.W.*

-Straße No.

GELD IST AN INTERNIERTE PERSÖNLICH ZU SENDEN	MONEY TO BE SENT BY POSTAL ORDER
UND ZWAR AUSSCHLIESSLICH DURCH POSTANWEISUNG	ONLY NOT PER REGISTERED LETTER –
– AUF DER RÜCKSEITE DES ABSCHNITTES IST DER	ADDRESSEE'S FULL NAME MUST BE WRIT-
VOLLE NAME DES EMPFÄNGERS ZU WIEDERHOLEN	TEN LEGIBLY ON COUNTERFOIL SLIP

DARLING MOTHER,

Many thanks for your letters, dated 10th and 11th of May. I was delighted to receive them, and would put you entirely at your ease concerning me and my work. My work is of the easiest kind : teaching elementary Latin, Greek and French, and learning Italian and a few other nice things.

Of course, the really great interest must, as always, centre in men and not in books ; in men who are in the same movement as yourself, and who draw you forward in your thought and in your feeling, and above all, in that deepening of the knowledge of—*i.e.* about—others which goes below intelligence.

Before I go on to trivialities I will give you

some news, which I have had to keep from you until I knew it as fully as I do now, since it would have alarmed you needlessly otherwise. F. U—n has gone to England, has joined the Army, and is about to receive his commission. There you have it all, and we may be proud. Myself, I have at times been frightfully perturbed, since the first news of his presence in England was a card from T., giving various vague remarks, which merely set my imagination working. Through the great personal courtesy of the censor, I was able to send T. a letter without delay, asking for immediate detailed information. I also wrote to Mr. U—n, telling him about my anxiety. Two p.c.'s came back from T., saying that F. U—n had joined the Army, that the medical exam. was stiff, and that his health was perfectly all right. Mr. U—n's long letter came the day before yesterday. He also puts me quite at ease about F. U—n. F. U—n evidently lived at " The Cecil " (in London, I presume) to start with, and then stayed with the T.'s in Lincoln. He then joined the 7th Batt. Wiltshires, and is at present training at Salisbury Plain.

My darling Mother, many questions will immediately rise to your mind, but the facts are now clear, and I repeat, we may be proud. Your letters show that you have been thinking of F. U—n a great deal recently, in a strain like that one which above all others has been borne upon me in this camp, and upon which, as a young man, I must base my own determinations for the future—namely, that "We rise out of ourselves above ourselves." F. U—n has been in England for about two months now, as far as I can make out.

Mother, I may honestly say that, since I know that all is going well with F. U—n, and that like all my friends, he is able to have the privilege of doing his duty publicly, I have grown much calmer, have been able to cast off a good deal of my nervousness, and feel strengthened in every way; God grant that he may be a help to others, and that whole-hearted service on his part may give him that humble dignity which it alone can impart.

On Wednesday last, the 12th inst., I gave an address at the religious service. It was the first time that I have given a religious address, and I called it, " Seekers after God," making it into a little talk on sincerity. Myself, I was not really satisfied, and thought that I had failed to bear my hearers with me, and the fact is that the form might have been much better. But if I am to be honest, I must say that I was pleased to hear from one quarter that some fellows had discussed it in their box afterwards, and to get various signs that, at any rate, some had been touched. Another man, until then unknown to me, has looked me up in order to get a copy. Since I did not write it out at any time, I shall make some notes for him. From a number of quite different sources I have been asked for the loan of a little poem I read. It is, at any rate, nice to know that you made some people feel. Another result was one of the most remarkable conversations I have ever had.

I must now turn to some direct requests. Would you oblige F. G. by calling at the Schwarzs', Verbindungsbahn 10, I.,* and sending, or having him sent the following things : white sun hat, straw hat, all the stockings, white

* The mother was still at Hamburg, waiting to learn if there would be a chance of seeing her boy.

flannel shirts, short summer underwear (*i.e.*, to the knees), and add to the parcel some face-cream and ink for both of us ? He apologizes for the trouble he is giving you. Please pay for the postage. We should each like a tin of jam. The things you have sent me recently are splendid, especially the *Schweinsfilet** in aspic. The tinned meat which you tried is very good, especially with a little sauce. Please send me some Worcester sauce. I shall write for some of my books through I.

Kindest regards to Mr. H. I shall be able to write to F. U—n, but shall not do so before getting a letter from you.

I am with you in my thoughts, and hope that you will feel as I do, and that in health and spirits you will feel thoroughly well and confident for the future. With all love, your

RICHARD.

* Fillet of Pork.

Absender:

Richard Roe.

Engländerlager Ruhleben

Baracke *13*

Box *16.*

2nd June, 1915.

An -To Mrs *Margaret Roe* — On *London. S.W.*

_____ -Straße No._____

GELD IST AN INTERNIERTE PERSÖNLICH ZU SENDEN
UND ZWAR AUSSCHLIESSLICH DURCH POSTANWEISUNG
- AUF DER RÜCKSEITE DES ABSCHNITTES IST DER
VOLLE NAME DES EMPFANGERS ZU WIEDERHOLEN

MONEY TO BE SENT BY POSTAL ORDER
ONLY NOT PER REGISTERED LETTER -
ADDRESSEE'S FULL NAME MUST BE WRIT-
TEN LEGIBLY ON COUNTERFOIL SLIP

MY DARLING MOTHER,

I received your letter, dated 29th May,
1915, a couple of days ago, and purposely did
not send my reply yesterday, since you wrote
that another was to follow, and I wanted to
answer both at the same time, but a delay in
the post can so easily occur, and I expect your
second note will reach me this afternoon.

Before saying any more, let me tell you that I
have no fear for the future. I cannot but
admire your courage, but let me warn you
with all seriousness not to expect too much from
F. U—n. My hope is that if he stays in his present
position, he may mould himself, and cleanse
himself to strength, like gold is purged in the

61

fire, but you must not expect all the process which you would ask him to perform, and which we think him capable of passing through successfully, to have been accomplished at the outset. Destruction is so easy, and building up is so hard. Help him, hope for him, pray for him, but do not set out to see the promised land before passing through the wilderness. Great things may be ahead of you; my prayers accompany you. . . . So again, though the germs of greatness for the future are there, and we must look to the progress of Life, while never allowing inactive cynicism to drag us down, remember not to look for the future already fashioned in the present.

I will just add one or two remarks about the practical side. I am delighted to read that you have been able to arrange money matters, and hope that the money at the bank will be placing you outside the realm of worry. I expect that you are leaving some of my money with Mr. U—n, so that I can write to him for anything in particular. But do not worry about those parcels from Holland, since Mr. U—n is now sending me all sorts of things, sufficient to keep me going, and I shall just write to Harrod's for some meat at times. Indeed, the stock that you bought will last a fair while. Please let Mr. J. know where my books, my clothes, etc., are, since I shall probably write for various things fairly soon. Don't trouble about sending anything these days, but simply attend to your own arrangements quietly.

F. G. sends you his kindest regards. His mother's address is Mrs. G—n, Ightham, Norton, Huntshire. I shall try and write to you, care of her, before I know of a definite address of yours, and you had better send her a note giving her your address as soon as possible. Have no worries about me at all. During the last fortnight I have at times felt real happiness, and in the immediate future I shall dispel the nervousness which would otherwise shake me up, by means of two things—concentrated work and friends.

I am glad F—d is here, and I have also met one of the most charming, dearest fellows you could imagine, one with whom I feel myself at one in feeling, and with whom disagreement is merely the disagreement necessary between two

63

minds aiming at the same end; one whom I know like I know D., with perfect confidence in the ground, the soil from which emotions, thoughts and action flow, so that I am able to judge all actions with a measure of truth, and able to look with knowledge to those actions which the future may bear. If you take this trend, the words disinterestedness, sincerity, friendship, love must bear the meanings of one chain, while the other trend will immediately consist in selfishness, disappointment, envy, hatred. Let us follow the first and give our best to the future. You shall know my friend's name later.

My thoughts are with you, Mother dear, in the hope that good may be in store for you, and that we may be able to do much in future, and look upon your present step with gladness and thanks.

With trust and love,

Ever your

RICHARD.

P.S.—You might write to M. to tell her that my duty-correspondence has taken up all my letters, and that I should simply love to have her French book.

Absender:
Richard Roe.

Engländerlager Ruhleben

Baracke *13*

Box *16.*

16th *June*, 1915.

An -To Mrs *Margaret Roe* ——— On *London. S.W.*

——————— -Straße No.———

GELD IST AN INTERNIERTE PERSÖNLICH ZU SENDEN	MONEY TO BE SENT BY POSTAL ORDER
UND ZWAR AUSSCHLIESSLICH DURCH POSTANWEISUNG	ONLY NOT PER REGISTERED LETTER —
- AUF DER RÜCKSEITE DES ABSCHNITTES IST DER	ADDRESSEE'S FULL NAME MUST BE WRIT-
VOLLE NAME DES EMPFÄNGERS ZU WIEDERHOLEN	TEN LEGIBLY ON COUNTERFOIL SLIP

MY DARLING MOTHER,

Many thanks indeed for your communications from Amsterdam. I am very glad to hear that you are feeling more comfortable, and that friends have been able to make your surroundings fairly agreeable. But the fact that no news has arrived from England is distressing, and I very much hope that you have something definite by now.

As regards my letters, I want to warn you so that you are not anxious in future: All letters going outside Germany are kept here ten days before leaving, and if this one reaches you earlier than could be expected under ordinary conditions, it will be entirely due to the personal courtesy of the censor. I am anxious to hear what news you have, and shall at the same time write to F. U—n to let both you and me hear further. I have not had a word from F. U—n himself since he has been in England. Communication is so difficult considering the fact that I have to write to you and Mr. U—n regularly. But by now he has had time to let you have news, provided my letter reached him ; but as I mentioned before, " 7th Batt. Wiltshire Regiment, Salisbury," is all I know.

Don't worry about me at all. I am in good health and Mr. U—n is sending me parcels. My friend's name is W. U. S., of Trinity, Cambridge, G—n's College. He is indeed one of the most charming men I ever met. We discuss, we talk and we work, we think and we feel, but we hardly ever oppose each other. Friendship may start from a common outlook on life, but it can only progress by unselfishness, feeling, direct and full, and intellect clear. What else can you want, provided you know that the former is the more important ? The fact of

The Spandau factories as seen from Ruhleben, with a barge in the centre and a German soldier in the foreground.

being a gentleman to the backbone is, of course, vital, but anyone whom you can call a gentleman must have just those qualities of feeling which I hinted at above, and must express in his life a certain attitude of altruism towards his fellow-men, rather than any outward formalism indicating conventionally good manners. To have a charming way of saying cruel things is one of the worst of all qualities. All the signs of good breeding, good training and good experience, combined with the fact that the acts and forms of acts which manifest these qualities, are the direct and immediate results of a trend of emotion calculated to produce them, and their type, and nothing but their type. This combination is perfect, and it is in proportion as you have found the true bottom from which a man's actions spring that you know him truly. If you know him like this, you know the tendency with which he will regard anything that meets him, and you will gain knowledge not only of the present, but of the future.

Facilities for doing work in the camp are increasing, and the entire educational work is being re-organized. This is, however, not the time at which to give details, and I shall write to you more fully about it later, when more has been done. From Thursday last to Sunday we had performances of the forest scenes in Shakespeare's "As You Like It." The music of the songs, etc., was written by V., C.'s music-master, very delicate, quite modern. It was as artistic a performance as you could have witnessed anywhere. The scenery, in particular, was most suggestive; simple green hangings.* However, I cannot go into details.

I shall try and get as much information as possible from England for you, but fear that I can do so little, since your letters will get there sooner.

Yesterday I got a charming letter from Mme. Laurent through Mr. U—n. She is doing official work in Paris, visiting the sick. She inquired after you, and spoke in terms of tender recollection of F. U—n, adding that she was glad to hear of his present occupation, since nothing could be better for him than that he should be taken quite out of himself.

Write me any news you get, Mother dear. I

* See page 236.

shall be with you in my thoughts. God bless you and send you happiness.

With every good wish and all love,

Your

RICHARD.

Your last letter was written on the 10th June.

Absender:

Richard Roe.

~~Engländerlager Ruhleben~~

Baracke *13*

Box *16*

22nd *June*, 1915.

An - To M~~rs~~ *Margaret Roe* — On *London. S.W.*

-Straße No

GELD IST AN INTERNIERTE PERSÖNLICH ZU SENDEN UND ZWAR AUSSCHLIESSLICH DURCH POSTANWEISUNG - AUF DER RÜCKSEITE DES ABSCHNITTES IST DER VOLLE NAME DES EMPFÄNGERS ZU WIEDERHOLEN	MONEY TO BE SENT BY POSTAL ORDER ONLY NOT PER REGISTERED LETTER - ADDRESSEE'S FULL NAME MUST BE WRITTEN LEGIBLY ON COUNTERFOIL SLIP

MY DARLING MOTHER,

Yesterday morning I got your express letter, bearing the date of the 18th inst. and the postmark of the 19th. I started to reply immediately, but thought it wiser to allow a day to elapse, and write with a calmer mind. In the afternoon a letter from Mr. U—n, written on Sunday the 13th at Guildford, arrived, so that I am glad that I did not send my reply to you off yesterday.

Let me give you my position without delay : There can under the present circumstances be no justification whatever for creating physical difficulties for yourself which will be insurmountable. From an outside standpoint I cannot feel that your godson's monetary difficulties are at all justified. You know my detestation of war and of all connected with its spirit, but when you join the Army at the present time, you do so in order to work, and for no other purpose. If F. U—n has been irresponsible now, I am very sorry ; and hope and trust that he will be able to show himself to his best advantage in the future, by giving himself wholeheartedly, and by bringing out those good qualities which we value highly through unselfishness. This will be a momentary difficulty for him, but if you create excessive difficulties for yourself, you will be less able to help him even in non-monetary affairs in the future. For your own position, quite apart from anything else, you must have certain questions answered as quickly as may be : Are you able to get at any and every part of the money lying at the —— ? Has the interest been paid regularly so as to accumulate during the time in which you could not draw it ? What possibilities are there of an impending lessening of the value of the capital ? Such questions as these must be answered before you can feel at all sure about your own position, quite apart from anything else.

Now, Mother dear, if he writes as you say, the best thing will be for you to go over and see F. U—n. . . . . Give him your love and mine, and show him that we look to him, and make him feel that we become great by making ourselves so small that we disappear altogether, namely, by working entirely for something greater than ourselves.

Many, many thanks, dear Mother, for what you say about W. U. S. and me. How sweet and feeling of you ? My thoughts are with you, and I only pray that all the good that you have done may bud forth to a harvest, that you can feel; a harvest it *is* bearing, and you need not despair of the result of any good action, though it may not be apparent at the moment. To-morrow will be the anniversary of our College ball ! What a year ! God bless you, dear, and give you strength. The difficulties will disappear as you meet them.

All love from your

RICHARD.

Absender:

Richard Roe.

Englänlager · Ruhleben

Baracke *13*

Box *16*

26th June, 1915.

An –To Mrs *Margaret Roe* — On *London. S.W.*

— -Straße No

OELD IST AN INTERNIERTE PERSÖRLICH ZU SENDEN | MONEY TO BE SENT BY POSTAL ORDER
UND ZWAR AUSSCHLIESSLICH DURCH POSTANWEISUNG | ONLY NOT PER REGISTERED LETTER –
– AUF DER RÜCKSEITE DES ABSCHNITTES IST DER | ADDRESSEE'S FULL NAME MUST BE WRIT-
VOLLE NAME DES EMPFÄNGERS ZU WIEDERHOLEN | TEN LEGIBLY ON COUNTERFOIL SLIP

DARLING MOTHER,

I got your express letter of the 22nd inst. on Thursday the 24th. On Tuesday the 22nd Mr. Morgan came to see me, and was very kind indeed. I had quite a good talk with him, and he was willing to do anything for me that lay in his power, but there is really nothing that I would care to ask. He did, however, take the opportunity of talking to the censor, and of mentioning the importance to us of the ability on my part to write rather more frequently than the strict rule allows, and both of us received the most courteous and obliging answer. This will please you, I know.

As to your action, I daresay it is quite the best you could have done, for I feel in how many difficulties you might involve yourself by going across without any real knowledge. But for my part, I had never thought of suggesting that Y——g could be asked to carry out such a mission. Unfortunately we have no one really suitable, and if he does his best he may be good and very helpful. He certainly has a number of good qualities, being very honest and certainly reliable. This I felt very clearly at Oxford. But as I mention above, he can, I think, be relied upon to give you some facts and is not likely to be borne away by a subjective view. This is very valuable and may be useful in practice, if he can get himself to write calmly and clearly instead of in that vague manner which he falls into at times. The future will show, and I am not pessimistic.

*　　*　　*　　*　　*

I only hope that you are not looking too gloomily towards the future, for I feel sure that the present difficulties are vastly exaggerated, and will come to a good ending. Our friend was as anxious for you as angry with F. U——n, and indeed I cannot blame him, for as far as I have any news at present, F. U—n's difficulties seem to be largely the outcome of irresponsibility. We may not give up, though, and must try to do our best and help in every way, and a great deal will yet be done. F. U—n has had much good luck of a superficial kind, but he has not had the real good luck of meeting a man of experience who could guide him and draw him out.

On Wednesday evening I had a quiet little supper in my box with this dear friend, whom you must almost (while I was writing this he came up to me) know by now. A delightful talk followed—indeed, it was one of the most beautiful evenings I ever spent. Yesterday it was Old Boys' Day at R—— and we arranged a meeting in No. —— box, consisting of a supper arranged by F. G., and music-hall afterwards. All this sounds fearful, and any supper arranged by F. G. is likely to be pretty good, but my own little evenings are simple, and their pleasure consists in being together with him, talking, and quiet (the other members of the box are kind enough to have their tea earlier then), and seated at a table with a white table-cloth, adorned by the daintiness of some white carnations—at any rate, such it was last Wednesday, though the flowers were not my own.

*   *   *   *   *

Now don't worry too much, Mother dear; the position of F. U—n may indeed be serious, but I have confidence that he will yet be able to show himself properly.

Excuse the handwriting of this letter; it has been written on my knee. I asked Mr. B. for some things, and had them sent without any trouble. Much love to you, Mother dear. I am frequently thinking of you, and hope you are not having too much bother about me.

Your loving

RICHARD.

Absender:

Richard Roe.

Baracke *13*

Box *16*

Engländerlager Ruhleben

9th July, 1915.

An -To Mrs *Margaret Roe* — On *London. S.W.*

_____ -Straße No._____

GELD IST AN INTERNIERTE PERSÖNLICH ZU SENDEN
UND ZWAR AUSSCHLIESSLICH DURCH POSTANWEISUNG
– AUF DER RÜCKSEITE DES ABSCHNITTES IST DER
VOLLE NAME DES EMPFÄNGERS ZU WIEDERHOLEN

MONEY TO BE SENT BY POSTAL ORDER
ONLY NOT PER REGISTERED LETTER –
ADDRESSEE'S FULL NAME MUST BE WRIT-
TEN LEGIBLY ON COUNTERFOIL SLIP

My darling Mother,

Your last communication which I have received is the express letter written on July 5th. The news has, of course, been hard, inasmuch as I feel what a blow it has been to you, but nevertheless, I am cheered by the beautiful, clear, direct and strong tone of your letters, and speak with all the earnestness which I command when I say that I am entirely at one with you, and urge you not to spend any money at present. On that point there can be no doubt left.

I am glad to hear that Y. T. has been so good, and that you have had help from his letters. Please give him and his family my kindest regards when you write. As regards leaving for England, it is no use rushing over anyhow, and you are doing very well to bide your time for the purpose of getting thorough information first. As for Mr. U—n's letter, it certainly does seem incomprehensible, but I have had a letter from him myself, saying that he has been thinking of the time we saw each other a year ago, and how now his aversion to my trip has been justified. He adds that it is perhaps as well for men to strive in their own way. My reply goes off together with this letter, and I have written to show that no sincere man ever tried to strive by himself, that the feeling of communal fellowship lies at the root of all deeply significant experience, and that it is in unity only, and not in divergence that we must try to work.

Your last letter was beautiful, and to talk with you like that once more seems simple and natural, and yet love is always something, which seems like a miracle immediately we try to look at it from the outside, while from the inside we cannot imagine it otherwise, for we are it.

No cheese arrived, but, rather a parcel with tinned fruit and chocolate. I have divided it,

and it has given very great pleasure. I had
W. U. S. in to supper with me to eat the fruit.
When I wrote to you about him before, I knew
him as well as I had ever known anybody;
since then I know him still better; all I have
got to know about him from himself has merely
contributed to deepen my love for him, though
indeed the view which you see at one part of
the road can never be the same as that which
you saw some hours ago, although the road is
the same. Through his sincerity he has the
most extraordinarily active and progressive mind
I have known intimately, and the potentialities
in him are tremendous. It is of no use for me
to thank you for what you wrote about him
and me; that you would remember him together
with F. U—n and me; for I feel it more than I
can say. And just a few days ago, quite a long
while after getting that particular letter of
yours, I read him that sentence. I also read
him parts of your last letter.

Yesterday I got the most extraordinary letter
in the world. It was from L. B., from whom I
have not heard for about eighteen months. She
writes that she and her brother have been

thinking of me very often, and that they are both longing to be able to talk to me again. This seems almost a miracle to me, for I have seen the brother only once during the past two years, and never written him a serious letter during that time, while I have only had, as far as I remember, two letters from the sister during the same time. Last time I was asked for some advice concerning the brother. It is wonderful for old friends to turn to me and think of me in such a time as this ; I feel that.

I am glad to think that Mr. Morgan is with you now, for he will tell you how well he found me, though indeed he saw me on the one day within the past month on which I failed to shave in the morning. I am thinking of the future and look forward to it with confidence. You will have done your best whatever comes, and I hope that it will not be said of me that I failed in giving what I could. Mr. B. and his family want to be remembered to you ; they have sent me various parcels, but I have now written to say that I am getting everything from England. Please give my kindest regards to our friend.

This is, I feel, a thoroughly bad letter, but I can do no better at the moment, and I am very anxious for this to reach you as quickly as possible. It is always a lovely thing to think of those we love and to talk with them, and since you have that special corner, what more can I say but that this letter is written in love?

RICHARD.

Absender:

Richard Roe.

Baracke *13*

Box *16*

Engländerlager Ruhleben

22nd July, 1915.

An -To M~~rs~~ *Margaret Roe* ___ On *London. S.W.*

_____ -Straße No_____

GELD IST AN INTERNIERTE PERSÖNLICH ZU SENDEN	MONEY TO BE SENT BY POSTAL ORDER
UND ZWAR AUSSCHLIESSLICH DURCH POSTANWEISUNG	ONLY NOT PER REGISTERED LETTER -
- AUF DER RÜCKSEITE DES ABSCHNITTES IST DER	ADDRESSEE'S FULL NAME MUST BE WRIT.
VOLLE NAME DES EMPFÄNGERS ZU WIEDERHOLEN	TEN LEGIBLY ON COUNTERFOIL SLIP

MY DARLING MOTHER,

Many thanks for your letters of the 10th and 18th inst. It is indeed good news that Mr. —— has paid the whole sum, and I only hope that this is going to be the beginning of greater calm and better harmony. He has certainly been writing to me in the nicest way, though one of my letters evidently was delayed, and in his last he said that he had not heard from me for over a month.

It is very dear of you to write of your pleasure in talking about me, and that at any rate I know, that you could have had no one more charming and sympathetic to talk with. You know without being told that I have in the meanwhile talked of you to W. U. S. We have had some

82

The Racecourse at Ruhleben, from the Grand Stand.

hours together at various times which in themselves, as mere dates, may pass from memory, but in their outcome can never die. If you have ever seen another who really feels something entirely new, giving expression to it for the first time, unable to find words at times because there are none, yet clear, definitely and directly clear, in his feeling, stretching, stretching, and giving forth what is only just within his grasp, then you will have seen what I have seen. If you have ever felt that you had lost the whole vitality of your life, namely religion, that you were sterile and dead; have then reasoned calmly on the consequences of this and compared them to the actual facts; have found that feeling and deadness were but temporary causes of what was to follow; and have finally emerged actually carried beyond yourself by the great positive force that you have found, then you will have felt what I have felt once. This occasion is, of course, definitely different from those mentioned above, and not the same. I will not, however, weary you with expressions which are too short to be understood fully by themselves, and for the clear expression of which I have no space at present. I have said enough to show you that the friendship is growing, and that the constantly increasing insight has served to increase my affection in the same measure. I cannot pay a higher compliment, if you understand me correctly.

There are many other things I have been doing lately, such as, for instance, teaching F. G. and I. boxing, but while there was a time when I actually took a keen interest in this sport, I now feel that my knowledge of a few tricks is a thing apart; like the blank sheet of paper inside the cover of a book, it does not add to the value of the book.

My thoughts are with you, dear Mother, but in the case of those we love, it is not necessary to think of them, in order that they should be with us. They are part of us, and we see the world enriched through them. I hope you are physically somewhat better than you have been, and that you are trying to spare yourself all excitement which can be avoided, while giving yourself as much physical rest as possible. If only F. U—n will take his present chance to breathe again, to be true to himself and to aim forward, how great will your happiness be, and how well deserved! Mr. J—ns has been very kind to me, and, I know, is able to rise, throw all that savours of controversy and pettiness away, as stuff for people who think that they have time for that sort of thing, and to see moral union as inevitably great when it is the expression of those who work for Life.

Please give H. H. my warmest thanks for his friendship, which he has shown again, and which is the source of real joy to me, and for which I would convey to him my most serious and genuine appreciation. You will, I fear, not find a letter of mine awaiting you in England, because I delayed writing on account of your prolonged stay in Holland. But I hope that this will reach you in Holland.

* * * * *

I finish this letter with a consciousness of its badness, of the inadequacy of what I wrote on the top of page two, of its failure to do justice both to him and to my own feeling; but I shall send it off as it stands, and my only hope shall be that your impression will not be too wrong.

In Ruhleben

Again, many thanks for your letters and cards.
Think of what we all feel—that you must not
make insuperable difficulties for your future,
and remember that I am always with you in love,

RICHARD.

Absender:

Richard Roe.

Englānderlager Ruhleben

Baracke *13*.

Box *16*.

26th July, 1915.

An -To Mrs *Margaret Roe* on *London. S.W.*

-Straße No.

| GELD IST AN INTERNIERTE PERSÖNLICH ZU SENDEN UND ZWAR AUSSCHLIESSLICH DURCH POSTANWEISUNG - AUF DER RÜCKSEITE DES ABSCHNITTES IST DER VOLLE NAME DES EMPFÄNGERS ZU WIEDERHOLEN | MONEY TO BE SENT BY POSTAL ORDER ONLY NOT PER REGISTERED LETTER - ADDRESSEE'S FULL NAME MUST BE WRITTEN LEGIBLY ON COUNTERFOIL SLIP |

My darling Mother,

I wrote you a letter to Amsterdam on Friday, the 23rd inst. While I wrote it I had apprehensions and doubts whether it would reach you in Holland; so I added " Please forward " to the address, and hope that you will get the letter soon.

On Saturday Mr. Morgan* came to the camp, and was kind enough to send for me. I thanked him for his kindness to you, and he said that they had all been fond of you in Hamburg, and you were a pre-eminently courageous woman, and had borne up well under all sorts of difficulties.

*   *   *   *   *

* American Consul-General at Hamburg.

My own advice to F. U—n, in thinking of his future . . . is let him be ready to put his whole power into all that he does, a power which is the impulse of working for the future at every hour and with every action, and is supplied by the knowledge that to be true to himself is to be true to his high self. There is one self only, and if we fail, we do so through the intrusion of some negating matter. We always have it in us to be true and help. F. U—n has much in him, and will have more, and he must go with the knowledge that both families will always be ready to help and are helping now, for there are other means of aiding than monetary gifts.

*   *   *   *   *

In the meanwhile, be sure that I am thinking of you. I am asking W. U. S. to write a postscript on the last page of this letter. You must know him pretty well by now, and be happy to feel that there could hardly be one who unites for me more beautifully the qualities of a friend than he who is with me now.

Every good wish, Mother dear ; my thanks

to H. H. and Y—g for their help to you, and love and prayers for you from

Your

RICHARD.

Richard asks me to continue this letter for him : if it were not that he assures me that you will not be disappointed to find another's handwriting depriving you of his own, I should be ashamed to curtail in this way the little space four pages allow for correspondence. Perhaps, however, my friendship for him will procure a pardon. We are, so he tells me, already to all intents and purposes introduced. You will know, then, the bond which the events of the last six months have formed between Richard and myself ; and I am sure that anything I can say of him will awaken an instantaneous response in your heart. He is full of kindness and self-sacrifice, ever ready to support the many who appreciate his sympathy, ever prompt to defend those ideals of which he is assured. He has proved himself fully alive to every opportunity chance afforded of helping his fellow-prisoners, and has never spared himself in his exertions.

Our first meeting was at a reading of Bergson's
" Le Rire," when he formed one of a circle
struggling against the numerous difficulties
which at that time obstructed any serious thought
in the camp. His presence was doubly welcome
—as a scholar and as an enthusiast. The
acquaintance then struck has ripened since into
intimacy. Impetuous friendships are liable to
a decay as rapid as their growth ; this tie, on the
contrary, has experienced a gradual and consistent
development. One day, so Richard informs
me, he hopes to supply us with a formal introduction. Meanwhile these few words perhaps
may serve as a link between us across the Channel.

Believe me, most sincerely yours,

W. U. S.*

* A Cambridge Undergraduate.

MY DARLING MOTHER,

Many thanks for your two letters from England. I am very glad indeed to hear that Mr. C. is so kind to you, and that your first weeks in England have been brightened by this good friend. Please give him my warmest good wishes, and let him and his daughter know that I am deeply appreciative of their kindness.

If you have not yet received my two letters via Holland, please write to the hotel to forward them. I sent them there to be forwarded just during those days when you were crossing, thinking that this would be the quickest means of reaching you.

Your letter telling me of your visit to Eastbourne—dated 2nd August—was full of the spirit of facing the present difficulties, and of reducing worries by meeting them, which I have constantly admired in you, and which, I hope, will be the means of much future help. Does the boy make any plans ? Has he something definite in view ? I expect not. The present disappointment to you is great, but the only thing is to work to help. " I hope the day will come "—so we have long been saying. Let us now say, " The day is here ! " We must do all that we undertake with the whole of our powers and the whole of ourselves. I look to the day when men shall have changed the present values, and shall find that happiness and pain, as they are at present understood, rest upon a morbid, retrospective view, and that love can never be vanquished, while fear is merely that state which we are in when overborne by materialism on our part, and confronted by greater physical bulk. To be true to ourselves is to be true to our high selves. Let us start by never saying anything we do not mean, and never doing anything which is insincere, and we shall end by being able to say everything that we mean, and say it well.

Have no fear, Mother. My thoughts have been with you and are with you in loving prayer.

F. U—n will have left now. If I am ever able to help him, I shall always do my best; now he has resisted, and it was not for him to carry out what we thought would be valuable. His life may be valuable in other ways. Ours must be valuable as we use it. I have written to Mr. U—n about you—indeed, he has got the letter, and I am now sending him another one which goes off with this one. I can only stand for one altitude, and can do no more than place it repeatedly before him and others. If you have noticed a more deeply optimistic tone in my letters from the camp than you have found consistently carried out by me before, it is in the main due to one man, of whom I have not spoken before, but to whom I owe more than I can tell. I can show it; I cannot lay it before anyone in words. His name is P—d, and W. U. S. and I are linked to him by ties of deepest friendship and respect. He is more than twice our age. It was he who was the centre of that little group into which I was introduced on my second day in camp, and which read Bergson's

93

" Le Rire " under the most extraordinary conditions.

I cannot say more about him now, but here is a beautiful mind. You shall hear more later.

My dear Mother, you wrote almost two months ago, that when you prayed for F. U—n and me, you remembered W. U. S. as well. Never was I more thankful to you, and, indeed, he is as fine a character as you could wish to see—sympathetic, adaptable, and consequently helpful. G—n tells me that his mother has written that you and she are going to meet. I am delighted to hear it, and hope that you will tell her from me that F—d is fit and keeping up his spirits well.

For the rest, my thoughts are, of course, frequently with you, in the hope that all your money matters are clear, and that the outlook is satisfactory. I am looking forward with eagerness to future news from you.

Please give Mr. H. and Y—g my hearty thanks for their friendship. I wrote to Mr. Morgan that you had arrived safely, and were staying at the house of Mr. C. He looked much better when I saw him last than he did some months ago.

Now, let us never allow our heads to droop ;

if ever we do, we rise the higher through recognizing how great was that part of our discontent which depended entirely on ourselves.

With all love,

Your

RICHARD.

Absender: *Richard Roe.*   Englänterlager Ruhleben

Baracke *13*   3rd Sept., 1915.
Box *16*

An – To M*rs* *Margaret Roe* ___ on *London. S.W.*
_____ -Straße No._____

OELD IST AN INTERNIERTE PERSÖNLICH ZU SENDEN | MONEY TO BE SENT BY POSTAL ORDER
UND ZWAR AUSSCHLIESSLICH DURCH POSTANWEISUNG | ONLY NOT PER REGISTERED LETTER –
– AUF DER RÜCKSEITE DES ABSCHNITTES IST DER | ADDRESSEE'S FULL NAME MUST BE WRIT-
VOLLE NAME DES EMPFÄNGERS ZU WIEDERHOLEN | TEN LEGIBLY ON COUNTERFOIL SLIP

My darling Mother,

Many thanks for your two letters, which made me feel more than ever how brave and courageous you are under all these difficulties, and how invaluable the kindness of Mr. C. has been. That F. U—n should have got into this further complication, owing to lack of consideration, hardly merits comment, and the sooner you can forget about it the better.

I am very glad to hear that you have been able to get into touch with the proper people to get those affairs settled, and hope that they are found to be in a thoroughly sound condition.

Of course I remember Mrs. N. Father and

96

you have often talked of her, and several books which have survived even to this day bear her signature, as presenting them to you and me. Moreover, I have a very clear recollection of staying in the country with her when I was quite tiny, but so small was I then that direct memory holds but one clear sunlit picture, while all the setting is lost in the fringes of a child's wonder, and the country itself has been turned into fairyland.

I have been very busy lately, and will tell you of last Monday evening, because I know that it will please you. The programme was as follows : " What's wrong with the world ? " The points of view of four British thinkers: M. S. Prichard : Explanatory . . . . R. H. Pender : G. K. Chesterton . . . . W. T. R. Rawson : H. G. Wells . . . . Israel Cohen : Israel Zangwill . . . . H. M. Andrews : G. Lowes Dickinson.

Each of them was supposed to have twenty minutes only, except, of course, the chairman, who confined his explanatory remarks to five minutes, but each went on longer. The object was to show the key to the constructive thought of these four men, and to give the point of view from which they regard present social and moral problems, together with the lines of practical alteration which they suggest or of ideal conception which they would follow. Rawson is a splendid organizer, so that every manner of difficulty was removed. There was no light, so that they had to sit on the platform under the kindly rays of five candles, while the audience of four to five hundred was left in the dark. It was, however, very patient.

Andrews was very humble about his contribution, but it will at any rate please you to hear that appreciation came from all sides. The fact, of course, is, that the author has some good things to say, and sees that the problem before men is not a problem of any exterior institutions, but one of morals.

Rawson's essay was very good. I read him the references which you made to him in your last letters. He sends you his thanks. I look to him to do great things in the future, as he is doing valuable work now.

One differentiation has forced itself on me with stronger and growing acuteness here at Ruhleben,

Prisoners at Ruhleben playing chess, with Barrack 13 in the background.

[*Facing p.* 99.

namely, the natural classes into which men divide themselves according as they have or lack the power of true friendship. For the man who lacks that power, the world holds the limited amount of meaning and value which a toy of extensive and complicated structure or a game of infinitely variable symbols and counters may suggest ; but he who feels the meaning of friendship and knows it in action, sees that values are opening out for him such as he can only wonder at, in the knowledge that the import of small things grows and of flashing intellect and bombastic self-assertion has disappeared, while he is creating standards by which those after him will be helped, and adding a positive force to the lives of those around him.

I should like to go on talking to you about this and kindred subjects, but space compels me to finish. You, dear Mother, have constantly worked for others, and your love is growing in the lives of those upon whom you bestow it. You are ever in my heart, and I often think of you when I am together with those about whom I have frequently written.

You can really do nothing for me as regards

parcels, for I am getting all that I could possibly require. I shall be thinking of you more than ever during this month, in the hope that your stay with dear friends will help to calm you, and drive away the worries which come from reflection upon the past, which is unalterable. The future is alterable. Let us be masters of that.

Every good wish and love from

RICHARD.

Absender:

Richard Roe.

Engländerlager · Ruhleben

Baracke *13*

Box *16*

2nd October, 1915.

An – To M rs *Margaret Roe* On *London. S.W.*

Straße No.

GELD IST AN INTERNIERTE PERSÖNLICH ZU SENDEN
UND ZWAR AUSSCHLIESSLICH DURCH POSTANWEISUNG
– AUF DER RÜCKSEITE DES ABSCHNITTES IST DER
VOLLE NAME DES EMPFÄNGERS ZU WIEDERHOLEN

MONEY TO BE SENT BY POSTAL ORDER
ONLY NOT PER REGISTERED LETTER –
ADDRESSEE'S FULL NAME MUST BE WRIT-
TEN LEGIBLY ON COUNTERFOIL SLIP

MY DARLING MOTHER,

Many thanks indeed for your dear letters, the last one of which reached me on Sunday last. I know that you have been worrying about me because you have not heard for a long while, but I am able to tell you that I am perfectly well, and have merely not been able to write lately. I shall try and let you have news of a kind, be it letter or card, at least every fortnight in future.

You have been constantly in my thoughts lately, and nothing could have been more welcome just on Sunday last than the news contained in your letter.

I will let you know what we are doing here. We have founded a social science circle, the members of which meet together every Friday evening, when one of them reads a paper, which is followed by a discussion. The first paper was read last night, on " Local Government and Social Reform." The chief interest lies in the fact that there are men here from widely different spheres of activity and experience, whose contributions are certain to be helpful and valuable to the rest, in putting forward new points of view.

Discussions are, of course, useless as a rule. You know how I hate discussion now, much as I used to love it. But it is clear that present-day actual problems must command the effort of each of us to help.

W. U. S. is secretary, and, indeed, it is he who has got it up. Myself I am going to write a paper on " State Education in Germany."

There is yet another circle which we are forming—or rather, which Mr. M—n, a young history don from Oxford, is starting. He formed the idea about two months ago, and several of us agreed to prepare papers. He has asked Andrews to be his secretary, and he has consented to fill that post, much to the disgust of his friends, who despise history in the ordinary political sense even more than I do. Indeed, the only thing worth studying, as far as history is concerned, are movements which have affected men's consciousness of things, and moulded their outer conditions by transforming their inner life.

Another activity in the camp which I have not yet mentioned to you is the Madrigal Society. This also was chiefly got up by W. U. S., and is under the leadership of a Mr. B—n. They have given two concerts, and we are very anxious to hear them again, for the choir is quite exceptionally good. The camp school also is flourishing, and has lately expanded so as to number well over fifteen hundred members. Classes in the most widely differing subjects, from marine-engineering to Celtic literature, are in progress, but the modern language teaching, of course, occupies the chief part.

I am writing this after hearing a lecture by P—d on St. Mark's, Venice. He had given it before to us in Italian, at a meeting of the Italian Circle. For to-day he had brought the last part of the lecture, dealing with his views on the function of architecture, into greater relief.

I was delighted to read what you said of P—d in your letter—indeed, you may truly be thankful. As for W. U. S., he and I are drawn closer together than ever. You, dear Mother, I think of you often when I am with him ; he exemplifies more than anyone I have ever met such honesty, sincerity, directness and whole-hearted giving of himself, combined with true chivalry. He can be relied upon, trusted and respected in every path of life, and will never fail to attract the affection of the best men with whom he comes into contact. My only hope is that his ability and gifts may always be directed in the proper channel, in such a manner as to subdue his faults, of which he is more conscious than anyone else. We are, I fear, usually so dominated by the standards and conventions around us, which we know to be artificial, rather than accustomed to follow our true feeling, and grow by convictions, that we deem it almost necessary to excuse ourselves when we feel along certain lines. I grow more and more assured that all really valuable work in the world is done by men with convictions, which act as an impetus as the result of a spiritual experience.

Mr. McLaren, an older man and great friend of mine, is likely to be in London fairly soon, and will write to you about me, so that you can get some direct news of my well-being.

My sincere thanks for their kindness to Mr. and Miss C. Please also give my kindest regards to Mrs. N. You will hear more from me and about me in the very near future.

With every good wish and loving thought,

Your
RICHARD.

Absender:

Richard Roe.

Baracke *13*

Box *16.*

Englanderlager-Ruhleben

20th October, 1915.

An -To M. *Margaret Roe* On *London. S.W.*

-Straße No.

GELD IST AN INTERNIERTE PERSÖNLICH ZU SENDEN
UND ZWAR AUSSCHLIESSLICH DURCH POSTANWEISUNG
- AUF DER RÜCKSEITE DES ABSCHNITTES IST DER
VOLLE NAME DES EMPFÄNGERS ZU WIEDERHOLEN

MONEY TO BE SENT BY POSTAL ORDER
ONLY NOT PER REGISTERED LETTER -
ADDRESSEE'S FULL NAME MUST BE WRIT-
TEN LEGIBLY ON COUNTERFOIL SLIP

MY DARLING MOTHER,

Many, many thanks for your dear letters. You write a little worried about me, and I hasten to assure you that my health is good.

It is very dear of you to send those things, which I am awaiting with eagerness, and please thank Mr. C. most heartily from me for the sweets and bag. It is just this change of something dainty that we appreciate above all else here, and nothing could be more welcome.

I will tell you a little more about my life here. The Social Problems' Circle is in full swing, and last Friday my Australian friend, H——, read a paper on "Casual Labour." He is at —— College, Oxford, and is a fine type of young Colonial, with extraordinary directness in outlook and in expression. W. U. S. is secretary of that circle. I still have to acknowledge the letter you sent to W. U. S. and me ; he was very thankful indeed to get it ; no one could be more appreciative than he of all that is true and real. Both of us are very busy now. Just as I write these words he comes in. He has a trick of always coming just at the proper time.

You, dear Mother, I feel you are still anxious that I should have gaiety and laughter. Are these acquired by seeking ? I do not value them as such ; what I feel to be of greater importance is to make people feel of those around them rather than of themselves, and they will feel the impetus to grow by acting, to expand by giving, instead of always making themselves the centre, and wondering what they can get out of others for themselves. Here in camp we notice the difference more than elsewhere, for we are in a circle. Those who are working, who are teaching, or in some way constantly occupied with doing what share they are called upon to carry out in the work of the whole, are usually easy to get on with, and easy to please, while those who are lazy or selfish are, of course, the everlasting grumblers. For my part, I must confess to laziness of late, but just at present I have plenty on my hands.

This is an exceedingly scrappy letter, but I am very anxious indeed that you should hear soon and have your anxieties removed. At the same time, I must say again that I am full of happiness and thankfulness to know that you are at the house of such dear friends. Again and again I think of you there, and would that I could thank Mr. and Miss C. for kindness which I feel more than any other. To know that you are there is to know that you are amidst real friendship, which is the greatest of blessings, and in surroundings to which I make bold to apply the highest compliment—namely, that they are not noticed consciously.

It is very nice of you to communicate with D.; please tell him from me that I am thinking of him at work at present, and am looking forward with confidence to the day on which I shall once more see him, the friend with whom I shared all that was finest and that is present with me now of our College days; my heart is with him, and my good wishes accompany him.

You will probably hear from a friend of mine soon, a Mr. McL——, also an Australian. He is full of quiet dignity, always speaking with the calm of mature reflection, and never going out of the way of a difficulty, while he is ever viewing those around him with kindly feeling and practising tolerance towards the honest efforts of others, even when his own results differ from theirs.

You ask me, dear, what you can do for me. But I can assure you that I am being looked after. A woollen scarf is perhaps the only article of clothing that I would suggest. I could have welcomed nothing more than what I am awaiting now. Again many thanks to you and to Mr. C.

Perhaps you could send me a copy of Congreve's " Comedies " (I believe that a cheap edition is published in the Mermaid Series) ?

Good-bye then, for to-day, dear. I hope that this letter will reach you soon, and find you in good health.

All loving thoughts to you,

From your

RICHARD.

Absender:

Richard Roe.

Engländerlager Ruhleben

Baracke *13*

Box *16.*

29th October, 1915.

An -To Mrs *Margaret Roe* On *London. S.W.*

-Straße No

GELD IST AN INTERNIERTE PERSÖNLICH ZU SENDEN
UND ZWAR AUSSCHLIESSLICH DURCH POSTANWEISUNG
– AUF DER RÜCKSEITE DES ABSCHNITTES IST DER
VOLLE NAME DES EMPFÄNGERS ZU WIEDERHOLEN

MONEY TO BE SENT BY POSTAL ORDER
ONLY. NOT PER REGISTERED LETTER –
ADDRESSEE'S FULL NAME MUST BE WRIT-
TEN LEGIBLY ON COUNTERFOIL SLIP

MY DARLING MOTHER,

Many thanks for your dear letters. I hope that you have received mine of the 20th of this month by now, which the censor was kind enough to allow to pass without the usual delay of ten days. Your letters have reached me regularly, and have every time seemed like a talk with you, or, if I may put my feeling into words more directly, to receive a letter from you is like the sight I should catch of one who is in the same room with me, while my attention is fixed on the work before me. I know that I am not alone, while I am working; I am able to work because I am assured of a feeling which urges me together with others to effort; occa-

The Promenade des Anglais at Ruhleben.

sionally I look up, and my assurance finds itself confirmed. Yes, there you are with me.

This would be the greatest thing, the greatest power, for making our loves serve their full possibility, this knowledge that our every act is embodying a particular trend of feeling, that every judgment is not a personal, purely intellectual weighing-up, but a joint living, loving, full expression of what fills our whole self. Then we should not be building up plans which have to be realized in detail, if all that sustains us is not to crumble down ; we should not have to wait for the great occasion or chance for which we have been scheming before what is servitude may become service, but every moment of our work will present the ability to use our instruments and service, while the growth that springs from it will be not the occasional attainment to a height to which few can rise, but the constant treading of a path along which all shall progress. I feel that to carry this out in our lives will be the only work which we can do if we are sincere, work which helps not merely by supplying certain comforts for the worker, but which adds to what is vital, namely, the sensibility of men to the call within.

On Wednesday evening I gave the address at the service here, the first week-day service there has been for some time. The idea which I meant to embody was that of " Religion as the impetus to sacrifice," but after speaking I felt that I had failed to say all that had seemed most real to me, as I had thought about it beforehand. But it is never any use worrying about what we have failed to do, and you can imagine my feeling of gratitude when a dear friend, to whom I had expressed a feeling of failure, left a note on my bed saying that for him, at any rate, I had not failed. This desire on his part to help me in this way is as charming an example of the way in which those who love act by making those whom they love act, and work ahead more freely, as I know. It was not meant to be a sign of what had been done, but purely a reminder— I cannot quote the note—that the value of any act consists not in outward success, but in inward intensity.

I have spoken before of H——, a fine young Australian. It was he who took the service.

Dear W. U. S. also wishes to thank you for referring to him in your letters. Mr. P—d is helping me in many ways, and, indeed, most of what I said on Wednesday came directly from his influence, as will also most of what I shall say next Monday about Education. By influence, I mean stimulus; but I must write about these friends later, since I have left myself no space.

I shall let Mrs. M. know of your well-being. If Mr. U—n has misunderstood my desire to help a poor sailor here, I can only ask the sailor to get someone else to do the same thing for him—which he will be able to do.

The parcel with the sweets and hot-water bottles has now arrived. I am more than grateful, and repeat that nothing could have been more welcome, and that a parcel containing a change like this one meets with appreciation such as you are hardly aware of in ordinary times. Many thanks to Mr. C., and kindest regards to him and Miss C.

Don't spend money on books for me, dear.

Much love, and every kindly thought and good wish from your

RICHARD.

Absender:
Richard Roe.

Baracke *13*
Box *16*

25th November, 1915.

An -To M~~rs~~ *Margaret Roe* On *London. S.W.*

-Straße No.

DARLING MOTHER,

The day before yesterday I received your letter of the 14th inst., telling me of Mr. McLaren's visit, your card, sent off the following day, and a letter from Mr. McLaren.

*   *   *   *   *

Our Hamburg friend* has written several times in the most charming manner. He is a real friend, faithful and true.

Many thanks for sending the warm things; they are very welcome, and come just at the proper time. Your Christmas present is charming; I am looking forward to its arrival, for the

* Presumably Mr. Morgan, the American Consul-General at Hamburg.

books will remind me of certain hours of friendship which I value more highly than any mass
of knowledge. The books have arrived this
morning, and I am able to say that you could
have chosen no better ones, and, indeed, that
the whole action, the idea and its actualization,
are typically feminine, or womanly, if you prefer
that word. We seem to want women wherever
a little imagination is required ; most men are
so used to act within definite lines, in fixed codes
not of their making, that the exterior rules
imposed on their conduct have become the easiest
channels for their thoughts. The symbols
influence the thoughts, if we act according to
rules, but the feeling will constantly vary the
symbols if we act according to feeling ; and it is
just this which most seem afraid to do—afraid,
apologetic, almost ashamed—so that when we
see someone assuming a particularly brusque,
devil-may-care attitude, we may be almost
certain that it is merely his armour which is put
on because he is ashamed to be true. The
remedy is to be true yourself, and he will see
that in your presence, at any rate, he need never
be ashamed.

In Ruhleben

Our Hamburg friend has written that he will write to Herr von S., and I am quite sure that all that is in his power to do will be done, that you could have no better hands into which to entrust anything you would like doing. He has written several times, and when I did not reply quickly, he wrote to the censor of English letters here to enquire about me. I have written to you repeatedly of my indebtedness to that gentleman, and he was again so courteous as to allow me additional correspondence with our friend.

Please let Mr. McLaren know that I have got his letter, and that Mr. L. and W. U. S. also have received letters from him. I am very glad indeed to hear that he is well, and from the bottom of my heart wish him all that is good. I hope this letter will reach you before you have sent the rug back, for I can assure you that I am well supplied with warm clothing.

I have much to tell you of what we are doing here, but must defer that to the next letter. Suffice it to say that I am now once more in the best of health and am very busy. The two are synonymous terms.

My kindest regards to Mr. and Miss C. I think of them often, of the charming house and its quiet, and thank them many times over again for their kindness. Mr. P. was glad to get the message from Mr. M. I shall write again soon, but close now.

All love and repeated thanks from your

RICHARD.

GESEHEN
M

Absender:
Richard Roe.

Engländerlager-Ruhleben

Baracke *13*
Box *16.*

20th December, 1915.

An - To Mrs *Margaret Roe* — On *London. S.W.*

_____ -Straße No.____

GELD IST AN INTERNIERTE PERSÖNLICH ZU SENDEN | MONEY TO BE SENT BY POSTAL ORDER
UND ZWAR AUSSCHLIESSLICH DURCH POSTANWEISUNG | ONLY NOT PER REGISTERED LETTER –
– AUF DER RÜCKSEITE DES ABSCHNITTES IST DER | ADDRESSEE'S FULL NAME MUST BE WRIT-
VOLLE NAME DES EMPFÄNGERS ZU WIEDERHOLEN | TEN LEGIBLY ON COUNTERFOIL SLIP

MY DARLING MOTHER,

There is so much that I have to acknowledge that I feel ashamed, and unable to express truly what I would. This letter will, I hope, reach you in time to bring New Year's greetings, but whatever be the day on which it reaches you, it will, at any rate, convey what I feel to be more important than all set greetings, the knowledge that throughout this period you have been constantly before my mind's eye. Above all let me say that it is a very great comfort indeed to be able to think of you spending Christmas at the house of our good friends, and that there is truly no place in which I would as gladly picture you. Dear Mr. C.! Please thank him for me for sending those things. He has a genius for sending exactly what is most welcome.

This letter has got to be very compressed, and so I am unable to say as much as I should wish, but he will understand without further details what delight he has engendered by the aptitude of his gifts.

I will first let you know how I spent part of your birthday, last Saturday. We had a meeting of the Historical Circle; the subject of the paper, if you please, was "Lewis II. of Bavaria," and owing to the fact that several members had considerable knowledge of the subject, apart from what is accessible to all, we had a very lively meeting. Afterwards I had the opportunity of reading with W. U. S., and you can imagine how glad I was to be with him on your birthday, finishing the day by being able to read and talk together without disturbance, a chance which is rare in winter. We then started Burnet's recent book on Greek Philosophy, which we intend to work through together in the so-called Christmas holidays.

I am very glad indeed that you have met Mrs.

S. From what W. U. S. has said, I know her to
be a woman of very great charm and beauty of
mind. Of her son I cannot speak too highly.
You will recollect, Mother dear, what I used to
write about him in the summer, and for the
present I will only add that more than his intelligence, it is his personal charm, and above all his
complete honesty, that has captured my heart,
so that I would oppose him with greater reluctance than anyone I know. He has never shirked
a difficulty. Of how many men could you say
this ? His perception of others is amazing and
being constantly concerned with what is essential,
he takes symbols at their true value, is never
deceived by what happens to loom larger in
the foreground, and having no regard for anything
but the spirit and the motive, could never be
bribed by the inducement of material or measur-
able success. A mother may thank God for the
possession of such a son.

All the things which you sent have arrived,
and each speaks to me of the personal care and
love which you have bestowed on its selection.
The box of sweets is splendid. I shall give
Mr. P. the books at Christmas.

22nd December. . . .

I have received your message through O.'s friend, and can assure you that on my part I shall do all that I am able to. In the first instance I had some doubts about the part which it was my duty to play, but I have none now. Mr. J. asked the boys to let you have his and their best wishes for your birthday and Christmas. Now they come too late for either, entirely through my fault. Yet you have been in my mind more than ever just these last few days, and I am full of thankfulness to you for all that you are doing.

I have not yet read Bourne's book in its entirety, and shall write you my impressions in my next letter, which shall follow quickly.

Yesterday evening the Literary and Debating Society had its Christmas meeting, at which, after a reading from the usual Carol, a number of men gave a Christmas message each, as representatives of the parts of Great Britain and the Colonial Empire. Mr. Prichard (not Pritchard) opened on behalf of England. My friend H—— spoke on behalf of Australia. I represented C——. I had been asked late, and

even as it was, the circumstances were peculiar.
After having tea with G—n, I entered a packed
hall, while the Dickens reading was just beginning. W. U. S. happened to be standing by
the door, and we two went out to talk in a box
close by, until a friend told us of the close of
the reading. I then joined the speakers on the
platform, and all of a sudden was called upon
to speak as the first of the Colonials. The only
word which I would repeat here is my conviction of the possibility of joining men together
through a common feeling which they carry into
their respective work, however different in
character. I hope that the time is not far
distant when I may be able to work more actively
and devote myself more effectively to you in
the spirit of true love.

Ever your loving

RICHARD.

My darling good Mother,

I received your letter of the 30th December yesterday, and my immediate thought was : I hope that you are still at the house of our friends. This is my chief concern and hope at the moment. My feeling of gratitude for what Mr. C., together with Miss C., has done is direct, spontaneous, immediate ; I would take both his hands in mine and thank him with all my heart. To think of you at his house has given me comfort and happiness, to hear from you was at the same time to feel the response, which true friendship must awaken. And, Mother dear, I say it with all earnestness :

123

You know as well as I do that the present state is no more than a temporary difficulty, and I hope that the time is not far distant when I shall be able to help very much more actively than I can at present. So I write frankly and without hesitation that I hope that you will not place any difficulties in Mr. C.'s way should he offer to help you at the moment. I am thinking of you constantly, and your letter makes me feel thoroughly ashamed at having saddened your Christmas, when you had made mine into a Christmas of love by all your loving forethought. I shall have an opportunity of letting you have a real letter in a day or two, which shall tell you of my plans here, and of the way in which I spent the holidays.

F. C. and G—n ask me to thank you for your Christmas cards, which delighted them. W. U. S. in particular has asked me twice to let you have a message of appreciation for your kindly thoughts and gift. He is a truly golden friend. Mr. P—d also thanks you for the books, and will write himself.

I am very anxious to ask the censor to let this letter pass quickly, and as the time for seeing him is nearly up, I shall close now and write at length in a day or two.

Darling, I am with you in thought and shall try to do all I can.

My best regards, my heartfelt thanks to the C.'s, and all love to you,

From your
RICHARD.

Absender:

Richard Roe.

Baracke 13

Box 16

Engländerlager Ruhleben

16th January, 1916.

As – To Mrs *Margaret Roe* On *London. S.W.*

-Straße No.

GELD IST AN INTERNIERTE PERSÖNLICH ZU SENDEN	MONEY TO BE SENT BY POSTAL ORDER
UND ZWAR AUSSCHLIESSLICH DURCH POSTANWEISUNG	ONLY NOT PER REGISTERED LETTER –
– AUF DER RÜCKSEITE DES ABSCHNITTES IST DER	ADDRESSEE'S FULL NAME MUST BE WRIT-
VOLLE NAME DES EMPFÄNGERS ZU WIEDERHOLEN	TEN LEGIBLY ON COUNTERFOIL SLIP

DARLING MOTHER,

I have now got your letter of the 2nd January, and am glad to know that mine has arrived. As for your Christmas parcels, which have not even yet been acknowledged in detail, not only did each part give pleasure by its particular aptitude, but the whole tone of my Christmas here was changed by their arrival. In your choice you have been able to pick not merely what was welcome, but what showed such immediate love that I felt you with me here; to you, of course, it seems all so simple, but to me, though indeed nothing could be simpler, it brought a message, to the answer of which I shall devote my life.

We spent our holidays fairly quietly here, as

126

far at least as my box was concerned, though indeed this was not the case with the camp taken as a whole, and no one could remain entirely unaffected by the spirit of roisterous and noisy " merriment." I spent Christmas Eve with W. U. S. alone, and on Christmas Day we had a little supper in our box, at which just the box companions and one guest were present. Most of the next days I spent with him, and on New Year's Eve was the guest at the table of my friends in the loft of Bar. 10, Mr. P—d, W. U. S., N., E. K., W. and T.

Throughout the days which required much tact and sympathy in many directions, W. U. S. showed himself ready at every turn. I would not say that he always does the proper thing at the proper time, since this implies that the mere act, the form, performed by anybody would be good, but rather that whatever one who acts honestly, through feeling, directly does will always be apt, suitable, devoid of personal assumption and helpful. Need I say more ? I know that Mr. and Mrs. S. are actively engaged in helping in a form which, whatever may be one's intellectual background, has always seemed to me to spring from a true view of what sympathy as opposed to formula actually creates in all those unmeasurable values, which alone constitute the real living content of our lives. I hope that you will see Mrs. S. again, and give her my kindest regards, while letting her know that her son is helping others to have faith.

You will be looking for a little news after all this time. During the holidays the Y. M. C. A. hall has been completed, so that there is now a large, well-lighted room, where many can read in quiet and freedom from smoke. The reference-library and several small class-rooms are attached to the big hall, which can hold about four hundred and fifty. Last Monday I gave a lecture to the German Circle on Heine. I very much enjoyed reading his prose writings, which I think show his 'cuteness, irony, and often his delicate *aperçus* even better than his verse, though as politician or thinker he must never be classed in the same rank as he is as a pure lyric poet, for his concern is always with the moment and nothing but the moment   An attempt at more, as in " Der Rabbi von

Bacharach," leaves us with the feeling, "What a pity! With an intelligence that pursues its course, how much might he have done!"

On Tuesday I spoke at the French Circle on "The aim of education." C., a college friend of mine, who is president, had arranged the meeting, at which P—r and I were the speakers. To-night P—d is going to read his paper on "Greek and Byzantine Ideals" at a meeting of the Historical Circle. I shall ask for permission to include a copy of the list of our meetings, which we sent to the members at Christmas, in this letter, so that you can judge of our activities.

P—d asked me to thank you very much for the books. He has read Bell's book, and wants me to read it, but disagrees with the theory. Bell, Fry and Lowes Dickinson are friends, and P. certainly is the P. whom L. D. knows. I am reading Bourne's "Ascending Effort" which you sent me. Its value consists in the remarks which lie apart from the main thesis. Some things he sees clearly—for instance, that science alone can never make for true progress, that the subject and the subject matter of a work of

Art are two quite separate entities, that growth must come from within ; but his thesis that the value of life is to be measured in terms of " choice ideas " is to me a start from the wrong end.

Chesterton's poems are excellent. Of course, clever, like everything he writes, but beyond that his love poems are true, his tone always dignified, and he always sees through cant.

You have been constantly in my mind, dear Mother, and I hope that you will be well when this letter arrives, and that you will be staying where you know that I love to picture you during this time, at which the transitory, passing nature of our present position is clearer to us than ever, but which has at the same time brought it to the hearts of all of us that we are making the future in ourselves, and that we can only work through love.

Please give my kindest regards to our good friends, and let them know that I often think of them. I hope that before long I shall be able to do very much more for you than I can at present. Again many, many thanks for all that you have done. I shall hope to hear from you again soon, and shall not give you anxiety again. I shall think of you constantly, and remain

> Your loving
> RICHARD.

Absender:

Richard Roe.

Baracke 13

Box 16

Engländerlager Ruhleben

21st January, 1916.

As -To M** Margaret Roe ___ On London. S.W.

_____ -Straße No _____

GELD IST AN INTERNIERTE PERSÖNLICH ZU SENDEN | MONEY TO BE SENT BY POSTAL ORDER
UND ZWAR AUSSCHLIESSLICH DURCH POSTANWEISUNG | ONLY NOT PER REGISTERED LETTER –
– AUF DER RÜCKSEITE DES ABSCHNITTES IST DER | ADDRESSEE'S FULL NAME MUST BE WRIT-
VOLLE NAME DES EMPFÄNGERS ZU WIEDERHOLEN | TEN LEGIBLY ON COUNTERFOIL SLIP

MY DARLING MOTHER,

I am writing to let you know that Mr. J. arrived in the camp yesterday. I was not unprepared to see him, since he had written to his boys a few days ago that he would in all probability be in the camp again soon. The day of his arrival was uncertain. Luckily I was in when the message came to the box, and circumstances combined to give us the power to make him comparatively comfortable for the first night. One member of our box is in the Schonungsbaracke at present, so that with his consent and the goodwill of the other members, Mr. J. could pass the first night in our box, to tide him over until a permanent place has been

132

found. All other members except one were at the theatre, so that I was able to bring the boys as well as him in to tea.

My impression is that he is physically in good condition, but the worries of the past months have clearly affected him. He is not very optimistic about his own future, but I feel that his energy, though temporarily suppressed through his state of mind, will show itself with all its old quality of vigour immediately the chance of work opens out a field for application. He says that he has not heard from his elder sister for some time. The day before yesterday he had received a letter from Mrs. M. telling him of Elsie's arrival. The father had gone to Holland, and found that the boat was delayed a couple of days, and arrived in a terrible storm. E. herself seems to be very worn out, and brings the sad tidings of the death of her smallest baby during the voyage. Of course Mrs. M.'s story of the negligence through which alone this calamity could occur, is harrowing, and her distress is genuine. The poor little child, after being thoroughly healthy, got a bad attack of diarrhœa (Mr. J.'s own baby died in the same manner). The whole trip seems to have been stormy and uncomfortable. Mrs. M. herself is now tending her daughter.

Y. B. is still in the sanatorium, and B. B. has gone back to the hospital, finding the house unbearable now that it is deprived of the son's presence. The knowledge will come to them, if not now then assuredly before long, that no mother loving her child ever worked in vain and that no deed which came from the heart was ever performed without avail.

*   *   *   *   *

I have received two letters from you during the last fortnight, that is since the Sunday before last, and I hope that you in your turn have in the meanwhile received my letter. Many thanks indeed for all your news. I hope that you will be able to meet Dr. W., for many of my pleasantest memories of school are connected with him.

My kindest regards to Mr. and Miss C.

All love from your

RICHARD.

D

Absender:

Richard Roe.

Baracke *13*

Box *16.*

5th February, 1916.

An -To Mrs *Margaret Roe* ___ On *London. S.W.* ___

_____ -Straße No._____

My DARLING MOTHER,

Many thanks for your letters and above all for all your good efforts. Before, however, replying to anything that you have written, I must let you know that, together with this letter to you, a letter to Mr. U—n is going off, in which I explain to him that my life being indissolubly bound up with yours, I cannot remain uninfluenced by your present position, nor without strain as long as there is the constant feeling of difficulty which I can do so little, seemingly little, to alleviate. I have asked him to help to tide over this time of difficulty, which, as I am well aware, is a mere crisis, a temporary worry, but which is a blind alley

135

in many ways, unless he is willing to step in.
You will not, I hope, consider this ill-timed,
for I feel that my own position must neither
now nor at any future time be open to doubt or
in any way built upon compromise. My life is
not going to be of any use to anyone, or productive of any work worth doing, if it is all built
on a lie, and you may rest quite assured that
whatever form the physical conditions may take
under which I shall be called upon to exercise
any efforts, they will not be acquired by a renun-
ciation of what is dearest to me, of you who have
never known what hesitation in the face of loving
effort on my behalf meant. There is no difficulty in the future for those who have faith and
it is no use for me to try and plan my life according to frames which will have to be changed
entirely; but one thing, at any rate, I can do,
namely, be true to the call within instead of
hankering after this or that particular form or
mould which someone else fills now, and which
in no sense bears within itself the value of the
man who fills it. Suffice it for the present to
say that our fears for the future are invariably
evolved by our worship of form and the threat

Ruhleben Racecourse : the prohibited area.

[Made at Ruhleben by Stanley Grimm.

[Facing p. 136.

to be deprived of that form. Let quality and motive take the place of quantity and " success," and those who kill the " success " will return home with shame in their faces.

I hope that you have by now received the letter in which I sent you the list of history papers. Last Saturday Professor P. read his paper on the " Philosophy of History." I was in the chair at that meeting, and shall have to preside again to-night, for the paper took the whole time and was so full of interest that owing to the suggestion of Mr. —— and Mr. P—d, we are devoting to-night's meeting to a discussion of last week's paper, instead of having a new paper. In the meanwhile, I have been able to let various members have the manuscript, so that the criticisms and additions should be valuable. The chief points of the paper were : (1) that the historian pronounces universal value judgments ; (2) that there is such a thing as the science of history, the epistemology of which is of course different from the epistemology (Erkenntnis theory) of natural science ; (3) that the evolution of history is the evolution of freedom. You see here the difference between

Philosophie and Weltanschauung, which has been put on quite a different footing by Bergson, and I think that it is chiefly from this side that the criticism will come.

Please be so kind as to write a few lines to M. C., saying that for the past three weeks, centering around her birthday on the 24th, she has been frequently in my mind, though I have been unable to write. I wish her all that is good and would love to hear from her some time.

My very kindest regards to Mr. and Mrs. H. and to Mr. and Miss C. I often think of them, dear good friends. W. U. S. asks me to thank you for sending him your kind regards and to return his own. I must close now, for I am anxious to send this letter off with special permission.

Have assurance, dear Mother, there never can be darkness again except in relation to light, to strive is to ask for more battles, the truth can never rest, the lover shall always fight.

Your loving
RICHARD.

MY DARLING MOTHER,

Many thanks for your dear letters, which, though they expressed anxiety for me, were full of hopeful news. In the meanwhile Mr. U—n has replied to mine, and is under the impression that you are well looked after. I have answered and told him that my concern is in no way diminished, and I shall continue to try to induce him to help in bridging over this time of difficulty. There is no lack of clearness about my position in the matter. Mr. U—n is constantly being exceedingly kind to me and is looking after me with every means in his power, but that can make no difference in my position towards you, and I feel none of your anxieties about myself. If I am unable to fill one post in life, I shall fill another, but there can be no doubt that my work and my position must in its reality depend upon the quality of feeling which I bring to bear on it, and I shall be perfectly content to mould that life and those outward circumstances which alone correspond to that feeling, rather than aim at some absurd form which someone else can present and take away. Take heart, Mother dear, the future has no terrors to those with faith, for they know that they will remain themselves, growing as they form and are formed by surroundings. The terror which the future inspires is always due to the fact that we imagine circumstances growing and ourselves standing still. In reality we also shall have grown when the time to act has come. There is no hope of my release for some time to come, and it will be best for you to make your arrangements accordingly. As you know, dear, I love to think of you at the house of our good friends, but if you think it better to go on to Mrs. M.'s, do so. Myself, I am grateful to Mr. and Miss C. in a manner that none but true friends can feel and impart.

The Racecourse at Ruhleben, showing the old fort in the background.

[Made at Ruhleben by Stanley Grimm.

[Facing p. 140.

Letters to a Mother from Ruhleben

The books of H. G. Wells have arrived, and have given much pleasure. I mentioned last time that we were having a second meeting of the Historical Circle, which was to be devoted to the discussion of Professor P.'s paper on " The Philosophy of History." The discussion proved so lively that yet a third Saturday was spent over the same subject, which last evening was occupied entirely by a brilliant presentation by Mr. P—d and Professor P. of their respective positions. Mr. P—d is exceedingly busy now, active and helpful in every department. In a fortnight's time I shall read a paper to the Historical Circle on Joan of Arc. Through Mr. P—d I have been able to read several works on her and must, at any rate, show my gratitude for coming face to face with this inspiring figure, who lived to serve and to love.

I am exceedingly anxious for this letter to go off now, and shall write you another without keeping you waiting long.

My kindest regards to Mr. and Miss C.

All love for you from your

RICHARD.

Absender:
Richard Roe.

Baracke *13*
Box *16*

Engländerlager Ruhleben

2nd April, 1916.

An - To M— *Margaret Roe* On *London. S.W.*

-Straße No

GELD IST AN INTERNIERTE PERSÖNLICH ZU SENDEN	MONEY TO BE SENT BY POSTAL ORDER
UND ZWAR AUSSCHLIESSLICH DURCH POSTANWEISUNG	ONLY NOT PER REGISTERED LETTER -
- AUF DER RÜCKSEITE DES ABSCHNITTES IST DER	ADDRESSEE'S FULL NAME MUST BE WRIT-
VOLLE NAME DES EMPFÄNGERS ZU WIEDERHOLEN	TEN LEGIBLY ON COUNTERFOIL SLIP

MY DARLING GOOD MOTHER,

Your letters have been a great source
of joy to me, and I am sorry to have to begin
once more with an apology for delay on my
part. In the meanwhile, however, you will, I
hope, have seen S., who is at —— College,
Oxford, and was a contemporary of D.'s there.
I did not see him often here, and he will not be
able to give you any idea of my trend or outlook
at the moment, but you will, at any rate, gain
some information about the developments in
the camp, and the way in which conditions have
been improved.

Your own affairs, however, are more on my
mind. I have been aware for some time past
that you are beginning to feel that your stay at

the C.'s is extending beyond its proper limits. You are the only judge of that, inasmuch as you are the only one affected immediately by the feeling of the C.'s; but for my part I should say that you would arrive at the best solution of your difficulties during the war if you could return to the C.'s after the trip which you propose, and remain with them until the war is over. You will soon, I gather, be in a position to use the money in London, the interest which is at present lying in London, and after that you will feel less constraint. But in all seriousness, Mother dear, I would ask whether you would not be in the most congenial company at the house of the old gentleman, and whether that would not give you the clearest opportunity of being of help to others. You would certainly be of help to Mr. C., and I think that your mind will be more at ease, that your outlook will brighten and change from within, if, after the bank arrangements are fairly settled, you are enabled to devote yourself and to focus your interest upon some work not concerned with what is usually termed your own affairs. In this connection I do not know whether you judge that you will be able to attach yourself better to some work in connection with Mrs. M. or with Miss C., but I feel that unless we have somebody we love whom we work for, that is, unless we be doing work, and that work come from our hearts, our life is fruitless, for our vision is limited. We must be sure that whatever we be doing at any time is just what it is best that we should do. Of all thoughts this is the one which more often than any recurs to my mind, that we only learn through love. Of course the feeling which produces a thought will be unique, unlike the feeling which prompts us to express the same words later. Those who hear us or are with us will know the change, and if we were perfectly sincere we should not even choose the same words.

I have not even yet told you of my paper to the Historical Circle on Jeanne d'Arc, which I read a fortnight ago yesterday. The writing of it has been a revelation to me. Of course, I am not interested in the politics of the period for the sake of historical knowledge ; what is really helpful is to have been face to face with this beautiful, sincere, pure, clear and simple figure, who by her truthfulness made those who compromise see how petty were their politics ; in whose presence all problems were clearly put, and therefore clearly solved ; who finally was arraigned before the united scholarship of the Church, and refuted all the catch-questions of the diplomatists. I dealt chiefly with her trial, since that shows her character better than any other part of her actions. Through Mr. P—d I was enabled to read Michelet's account, as well as the biography by Anatole France, and G. Hanotaux's book. I managed to get several other books, but almost all my work consisted of French reading. Mr. P—d kindly took the chair for me. I read my paper to him beforehand, and he took the trouble to write an account of his own conviction as regards Jeanne d'Arc, of his admiration for her, and of his visits to the different scenes of her action. He raised the tone of the discussion to a level which no one else could have stimulated. W. U. S. gave the truest help by asking the question which showed that he alone has really seen the issue, and in my foolishness I gave a history of theories about Jeanne d'Arc as an answer.

Please give my kindest regards to Mr. McLaren. I very often think of him, but he knows that I cannot write. If you will let me have his address, I will try and send him a card. I hope you will see Mrs. S. again.

I am feeling happy because I am once more feeling the love which alone can show us light for some short distance ahead on the road, which without it remains dark. You shall be happy, my dear Mother, for you also shall know in future, as you have taught me since I was small, that in religion and in love, that is, when we are in harmony with the spirit of life, we relinquish the domain of probability and grasp firmly those values which have become a certainty.

Many thanks for all your good efforts. Mr. J. lives at Baracke 3, Box 6, and is pretty well. He sends his kindest regards.

Love from your

RICHARD.

MY DARLING MOTHER,

I have received your letters of the 15th and 18th April, and, though it may seem cruel to you, I am delighted that you have been prevented from going to Holland at the present time, for the journey under existing conditions and, above all, a stay for an indefinite period at a place of uncertain safety for the sake of dubious advantages seemed to be alarming rather than otherwise. I hope that it will be possible to arrange the financial affairs without leaving England, though later the traffic may become more regular again and then a journey will well repay the trouble. For the present, however, I am glad that you are going to remain in England. It will be best not to interfere with Mr. U—n's arrangements as far as the sending of parcels is concerned, for he has organized the supply in a charming way and by additions from time to time has met the changing needs of camp life here with a kindness and a desire to do all in his power for me which is beyond thanks. But there is no doubt whatever that an occasional parcel from a lady, be it never so rare, like, still better, a letter from a lady, is full of a quality of imagination and the insight of sympathy which a man only rarely even aspires to. Only yesterday, as I spent an odd quarter of an hour in the latter part of the day turning over the leaves of a book in the library, I came across the photo of a woman, which awoke an immediate sense of the loss we suffer here through the lack of the companionship and help of women. The presence of elements which tend towards materialization in the worst sense of the word, namely, a worship of form and judgment by weight, is overwhelming in the case of those who have not felt the influence of women so as to have been moulded to think and feel as the women themselves. If we were to look

A football match at Ruhleben

[Facing p. 148.

into the hearts of most men I know that we should find that they have at some time been influenced through action by someone who, as they realized, had travelled further along the road which they themselves were treading at the time, and the thought will often occur: "At any rate, in 'his' or 'her' presence there cannot exist any selfish motive, any mean desire, or any impure thought." The personal centre of influence seems to have embodied Life itself, and here to me lies the explanation of the constant desire of men to individualize the spirit of Life, to make a personality of God, and to love—the pure mirrored picture of our "sentimental" tendencies as the friend who beckons and rewards our efforts by the trust of a further and higher task, and to fear it as the judge whose verdict is unerring because he knows us as we alone know ourselves, for he is the focus of our own impulse to create.

You need have no fear of the future. The question which we should put before ourselves —and the need of a deliberate question is already the sign of imperfection—is not, "What will come out of it?" but "Is it right?" Now in the lives of most of us a woman or women rather than men have been effective in inspiring us with the sense of our own value as instruments of something which unites us to others, but never as ends in ourselves. That is why those whose childhood and later life was spent in friendship with their mothers or in love which grew through looking ahead instead of aside, have here retained the qualities of insight, sensibility, freedom from all pretentiousness which must always win the hearts of others. I hope that you do not mind this long sidepath which tells you nothing concrete about my life here, but it is a delight, good Mother, to talk to you again, and I have made no effort to resist the temptation of expressing these few thoughts.

The summer term has begun and we are all busy at our various work, though it is too often scattered and incoherent. I notice that my thoughts about women started with parcels, and I need hardly repeat that I should not like you to spend much money on sending me things, but that occasional dainty supplies such as those chocs, which gave unmeasured pleasure, are exceedingly welcome.

I have read Chesterton's poems a number of times, and have even to-night lent the volume to my friend F—t of Bar. VII., of whom I have spoken before in connection with the History Circle. It is a delightfully refreshing collection and certainly contains some of the best writing I have seen since the beginning of the war.

God bless you, Mother dear. As I sit here the world seems vaster than ever it could have seemed before, while all life seems to be reduced to the simplicity of the gnosis " I know," yea " I believe."

Ever your loving
RICHARD.

Absender:

Richard Roe.

~~Tagiladerlager~~ ~~Ruhleben~~

Baracke *13*

Box *16*

13th May, 1916.

An – To Mrs *Margaret Roe* — On *London. S.W.*

————————————————— -Straße No.———

GELD IST AN INTERNIERTE PERSÖNLICH ZU SENDEN	MONEY TO BE SENT BY POSTAL ORDER
UND ZWAR AUSSCHLIESSLICH DURCH POSTANWEISUNG	ONLY NOT PER REGISTERED LETTER –
– AUF DER RÜCKSEITE DES ABSCHNITTES IST DER	ADDRESSEE'S FULL NAME MUST BE WRIT-
VOLLE NAME DES EMPFÄNGERS ZU WIEDERHOLEN	TEN LEGIBLY ON COUNTERFOIL SLIP

MY DARLING MOTHER,

My other letter clearly tells you nothing concrete, and I hasten to supply, at any rate partially, what is lacking. You will have heard of the death of Mrs. H.'s grandfather. I sent Mrs. H. a letter in your name as well as in my own and addressed it to ——, which I hope has been the means of, at any rate, letting her know my sympathy.

Here our course of lectures on " The Development of Germany " has begun, and though the worth of the different lectures will certainly vary considerably, I am confident that the series as a whole will be productive of good. My own contribution of lectures on Napoleon is fixed for the beginning of July. Most of my reading in connection with these lectures is of course in German, and I am taking Treitschke above all and Meinecke as foundations. With Treitschke I frequently have a feeling of resentment, as if I were being shouted at rather than spoken to. Some time I hope to possess full competence to judge him and the movement of which he is the guiding star in historical presentation, though it is by no means confined to history, but finds its expression in the voluntarism of philosophy and that regard for the technical accomplishment of commercialized science which will assuredly be changed into the advance of men with the aid instead of under the banner of science. I shall do much more historical reading in the near future than I have done in the past, for abstractions which are accompanied by my own dislike of the trickery of philosophical clap-trap are only too liable to turn into generalizations which serve as a cloak for lack of knowledge.

Dear T. in my box has added greatly to my comfort, and above all given me immense pleasure by adding yet another long shelf above my bed.

You know my habitual untidiness, Mother; well, now, at any rate, all is well arranged. T. is an artist; not that I mean to convey my appreciation of his musical gifts, which no one would dispute, but his insight is gained through feeling rather than analysis, and he often sees much truer than others of keener intellectual powers. His modesty as regards his own judgments or opinions is almost ludicrous. He always sees the essence of what you are saying or thinking, and himself feels such problems only as are true difficulties, instead of the superficialities beyond which others of analytical temperament never seem to pass. In the box I find myself almost invariably in agreement with T., and when we disagree, it is the disagreement which one feels in the case of those who work with unselfish, generous chivalry, and which we know to be formal only.

I have mentioned F—t before; he is intellectually the most brilliant boy here; but I am fond of him for other reasons than those of mere literary interests or common applications. He is one of the most cheerful, bright, witty and spirited companions I know, while his chaff never conveys ill-feeling, because it is never bitterly directed.

His nationality is Welsh—as that of two other F—t's, of whom more later—but he speaks French like a Frenchman and German particularly well. To-night at the History Circle, M., who lives with F—t, read us a paper on " Milestones in the Development of the Canadian Constitution." M. is a young Canadian musician of extraordinary ability as a conductor. While F—t is very talkative, M. speaks but rarely, and then in a good-humoured, slow manner, and always contrives to contribute to and help the conversation or the silence—whichever it be— by his short phrase, or even by a look, which shows that he has been thinking and which forces those with him to take note. He is a charming fellow.

Only a few days ago I received another letter from Mme. Laurent ; the dear good friend writes from her flat at 7 Rue de Jouy in her usual intimate, delicate and, above all, feeling and loving manner. I mean the word loving in its only true sense of an expression which provokes the same trend of feeling which engendered it. Every time she inquires after you and never forgets to say that she has been thinking and even talking of F. U—n. Few signs of friendship have affected me so much as this series of four letters, spread over nearly a year, while I myself have not written once. Only too often it is the pupil, not the master, who is forced to say : O thou of little faith, couldst thou not wake with me one hour ?

The summer is upon us now, Mother dear, and beyond all spaces, there is in my heart the assurance of that transcending love which we can only submit to in others, and as we bow, pray for strength to act ourselves to continue the love which was never deserved.

Ever your loving

RICHARD.

[*Made at Ruhleben by Stanley Grimm.*

The Grand Stand, with a Rugby football match in progress.

[*Facing p.* 156.

MY DARLING MOTHER,

Many thanks for your frequent letters, which have kept me not merely informed, but made me almost a participator in your life. In the meanwhile you will have received my letters and gathered from them what I am doing here. Let me just reply, however, to your words about W. U. S. I asked S. to look you up in the hope that you would gain some knowledge of the organization of the camp life, the material improvements, the different societies and other means of joining men of common focus, which I have hardly ever described and which might add to your mental picture of the physical outlines of our activity here. . . . I will not now dwell on the impression which I gained from what you write of S., but will just add a word about W. U. S. I notice that when I think of the future of some among us, I invariably bring to mind certain definite things which these individuals have done or produced in the past, and conclude that he who could bring forth such a thing will with further training create what will be much finer.

Of these it might be said that they have no future, but rather a great past before them. With others the case is reversed : To think of them at all is to think of what they are becoming ; not of this lecture or of this article which they wrote, but of this spirit in which, through which they do everything which they do ; and then to know in our hearts that wherever that spirit shows itself, there love the creator speaks.

Of W. U. S.'s failings I may at times become aware, but to you, dear Mother, I need hardly say that I would willingly entrust to him what I cherish most dearly, and that his course appears to me as a constant advance, though never as a formal progress of events. You would think that relationships had a tendency to become stereotyped when you had lived well over a year in the same box with four others, but such is far from being the case. I may, indeed I am sure I have, written about H. T. before. He is as unselfish a person as one may well conceive. You will remember that he is a professional pianist, and being an artist in every fibre he has above all that supreme gift, the lack of which one is sometimes tempted to associate with the unpardonable sin, the feeling for atmosphere. We have been drawn very close together latterly, and he has endeared himself to me by the purity of his mind, the delicacy of his feeling, the sincerity of his self-devotion, and that unwearying effort and unswerving direction of all his acts by the inner harmony which is a daily, a constant spring of love for me. He is the only member of the box who never offends your taste and never hurts your feeling, but whose life is an encouragement to act. I almost think that the only advice I could give to anyone now would be : Go and love, and all shall be added unto thee. Find someone ; he will probably already be in the same room.

Up to this point I wrote several evenings ago,

and would not now alter what I put down then, and may not add, for lack of space forbids. When Mrs. H.'s grandfather died I wrote her a short letter, thinking that you would like her to receive a sign that she was being thought of. She replied with a beautiful letter, in which she spoke of the effect of her grandfather upon her own life and the encouragement which his life has exerted. Of course she was deeply affected; yet she wrote with hope about her sons, and about the outcome of the present war in a spirit which is, alas, rare at the moment, but which will astonish us all, I feel, when we see where we have moved to in ten years' time. We cannot be neutrals now. We are all fighting against ourselves, and we are all fighting for ourselves.

Mrs. H. was delighted to hear about you, and should you like it, I will write to her again to let her know about you.

I am glad to hear that you are meeting Mrs. Maddison and her friends; please remember me to her when next you see her. You wrote that you were going to a concert of her songs. Was she pleased with it? It is a delight to read that you have met new friends through her.

Mrs. S. wrote to W. U. S. that she was asking you to stay a week-end at her house. I hope that you will be able to do so. Only to-day I received your dear letter of May 18th, and felt sorry for not having sent the present letter off earlier, though your reproach comes in the gift of love.

Sunday before last I gave a little lecture in Italian on " Autobiographical Literature," though many errors had to be corrected before I read it.

On Wednesday last W. U. S. read a paper on those poems of Chesterton, a copy of which you sent over for Christmas. It was a poet's paper. Not a fit subject for criticism.

As I close you are nearer to me than ever ; the infinite is with me and that silence which is more full of meaning than any storm ; good-night with all my heart : may it be good-morning when this letter reaches you.

Kindest regards to Mr. and Miss C.

Your loving
RICHARD.

MY DARLING MOTHER,

This moment I have received your dear
letter dated May 31st, and my remissness was
again brought home to me by this, the last of
a series of letters written by you during a time
when you received no news whatever from me.
What these good, loving signs of your thoughts
have been to me while working in a rather irregular
manner here, I can at the moment express only
by saying that you have made me continue the
path of what *I know to be right* in preference
to what I thought might please, and that you have
indued me with the spirit to continue* in several
courses of action though the visible result remains
outstanding.

* Refering to his release.

162

In the meanwhile I have been finishing my two lectures on Napoleon, finding of course, as usual, that you are constrained to give in an hour what you would prefer to write in a number of volumes. How easy it must be to write big books !

I told you in my last letter that I had changed the character of my French class, and started a small group of men, who had done some work before and would advance quickly, at the beginning. Several of my friends who speak French well and love it, have now undertaken to give fortnightly lectures to my class. Members of other classes will be able to attend on those mornings. My chief aim is to make others feel that their study of French is leading them towards something which nothing but France can give, and that they can already make French thought a living help. Next Saturday week C. is going to begin with a lecture on Stendhal, to be followed a fortnight later by F—t on the Touraine. It may seem at times as though we were thoroughly cut off from the real workers here, as though we had been placed in a backwater, with the permission to go to sleep, or maybe read, if we preferred, without any ability to affect the wider struggle which was being waged during our doze. But I have previously written to you that this war seems to me the opening for the greatest leap forward which life has ever accomplished, and that I feel it to be not a clashing of opposing group-selfishnesses, but an united cleansing of our conscience from that attachment of value to matter to which each is prone.

After I had just finished this sentence two interruptions occurred. The first a conversation with dear H. T., who was sitting alone with me in the box. I love him for his difficulties, for they are the doubts of one who sees the shadows only because he is advancing with the light and who acknowledges the light of others because he is as yet in darkness. The other break was caused by I., who came to bring me his French work. His progress has been astonishingly quick, and, after about six weeks' work, he has, besides doing regular work for me, been able to read a number of good French books, and I am confident that he will enter into the language well.

There are two favours I would ask of you,

Mother dear. Firstly, please write some message in your next letter which I may copy for Mr. B., from whom you tell me you have heard and who would, I know, be overjoyed to receive some thought from you. Secondly, please send me the autobiography of Loisy, the French theologian. Mr. P—d had told me of it long ago, when I was unable to get it. It is a small book and would probably have to be ordered from Paris.

Mr. J. is looking rather better now than he did some time ago. I do not see him constantly, or even daily, for our spheres of action are different and one meets but few except those with whom one's activity forms a natural link.

How is Mr. C. ? I often think of him and in re-thinking the past it seems to me that the occasions on which I have been together with him are not very numerous, but that each is distinctive and individual, and remains indelibly impressed upon my mind. Let me renew my expression of gladness at the knowledge that you are at his house and that you have found such charming friends.

Our friend will have written to you that I

am well; physically healthy, and as for reality, who ever dared say a happier word than that he had friends ? Good mother, if you have had to wait for long, forgive me. Again, all my thanks for continuing to write.

My kindest regards to Mr. and Miss C. Please tell Mr. McLaren that I often think of him and that his book on German education which he left me has helped me considerably in preparing my lectures. To those whose love continues, even the dead may turn and bow, and though the rose might marvel at the sweetness of the breeze, she would not quench the perfume she exhaled.

Love,

RICHARD.

E. G

Absender:
Richard Roe.

Englänferlager Ruhleben

Baracke *13*
Box *16*

28th August, 1916.

An - To M.... *Margaret Roe* .... On *London. S.W.*

....................-Straße No........

GELD IST AN INTERNIERTE PERSÖNLICH ZU SENDEN | MONEY TO BE SENT BY POSTAL ORDER
UND ZWAR AUSSCHLIESSLICH DURCH POSTANWEISUNG | ONLY NOT PER REGISTERED LETTER -
- AUF DER RÜCKSEITE DES ABSCHNITTES IST DER | ADDRESSEE'S FULL NAME MUST BE WRIT-
VOLLE NAME DES EMPFÄNGERS ZU WIEDERHOLEN | TEN LEGIBLY ON COUNTERFOIL SLIP

MY DARLING MOTHER,

Letters have followed upon letters, and you in your turn have had so extraordinary a wait that I cannot send an apology which shall seem adequate, and must ask you to be kind again, though I pass beyond seventy times seven times in my failures. Through the great courtesy of the censor, this letter will reach you quicker than others, and I am anxious to write you first of all what I wrote to Mr. U—n a couple of days ago.

*   *   *   *   *   *

Such news as I can give is, I fear, all ancient history, but it shall not be spread out too far.

In Ruhleben

My lectures in the early part of July on Napoleon went off quite well, since they gave me the opportunity of centring most of the criticism in particular men as focuses of a movement. One other incident may interest you. The two educational bodies in the camp, the Camp School and the Arts and Sciences Union, had had a quarrel, which finally burst into flame at the school teachers' meeting on the 5th of this month. The atmosphere became so heated and there seemed to be so little chance of an adjustment at the meeting that an advisory committee was formed, to whom the two respective committees might refer their difficulties. M—n refused to be a member, and those elected were P—d, Mackenzie and Andrews. You may know of Mackenzie. He was a friend of P.'s. So salutary was the mere existence of this committee that most of the difficulties, and certainly the acute ones, were got over in a week.

Of course the rumours about exchange agitated many, and particularly in the middle of last month we passed a few days in which there was no possibility of remaining unaffected by the general unrest. I am told that two exterior signs of this unsettled condition were a marked slackness in school attendance and a sudden rise in the number of tins brought to the boiler-house to be heated.

Mother dear, there are some good friends here who have made the earth seem golden and have brought eternity into the present. But it is difficult, it is impossible to sever understanding from art. Dear H. T. and W. U. S. are two such friends. All true reward comes with original swiftness, and at times some men seem more beautiful than you could have imagined anyone being. It is at such moments that we feel the love that tried to hide itself, the tenderness that came unsought. When I think of the few things I really know, I am forced to acknowledge that they reduce themselves to the experiences of a few seemingly isolated instants when insight was granted after love had been expended. Indeed it would not be too much to say that all that constitutes our present understanding is the sum of the love we have given in the past.

W. U. S. is a true genius. To say this must seem extravagant to many ; with me it is but the expression of such confidence and sympathy as he has gained, nay more, won, conquered for himself against many difficulties. H. T. is not so widely gifted, nor has he the intellectual grasp of W. U. S., but nothing could surpass the beauty of his mind, and he has never given unnecessary pain. Imagine what it means, Mother, to be able to say this of one with whom you have been living for a year and a half in a horse-box shared by three others. The value of P—d's friendship is inestimable. His experience of the world seems the least part. It is rather that he is forever urging forward and has never given up the struggle. With him a true experience finds ever-ready sympathetic insight. Perhaps it requires an internment camp to teach the value of tact. I never met anyone so conscious as W. U. S. of the response which others make.

H. T. has got up a couple of Chamber Music Concerts, at which he will lecture on the development of Chamber Music.

I am feeling more than apologetic for this very scrappy letter, but shall send you another very soon, and hope that this one may at any rate serve to remind you that at those times when all the earth seems clothed in the garment which heaven only could rightly wear, you are not far away.

Your loving

RICHARD.

" I wonder, if many of us will miss,
　　When the day of freedom dawns,
　This Camp, which like a chessboard is,
　　Whereon we are but pawns ?

" Sometimes a pawn is taken away
　　For hours—at least twenty-four !—
　And when I think it over, I say :
　　I don't want to play any more."

From " In Ruhleben Camp."

PART II

CHAPTER VI

THE CONDITIONS OF RUHLEBEN CAMP

SOME years ago Sir J. M. Barrie gave us, among the farces with which he periodically conjures thousands from the pockets of the English, a play called "The Admirable Crichton," brilliantly written, brilliantly acted.

In it a yachting earl and his family and his guests are shipwrecked on a desert island. The butler, being the most capable person in the party, assumes the dictatorship, and the various members of the aristocracy become hewers of wood and drawers of water and (the ladies) domestic attendants.

Something very analagous to this has happened on a fashionable racecourse in a suburb of Berlin, where a number of English prisoners, with, very appropriately, an earl among them,

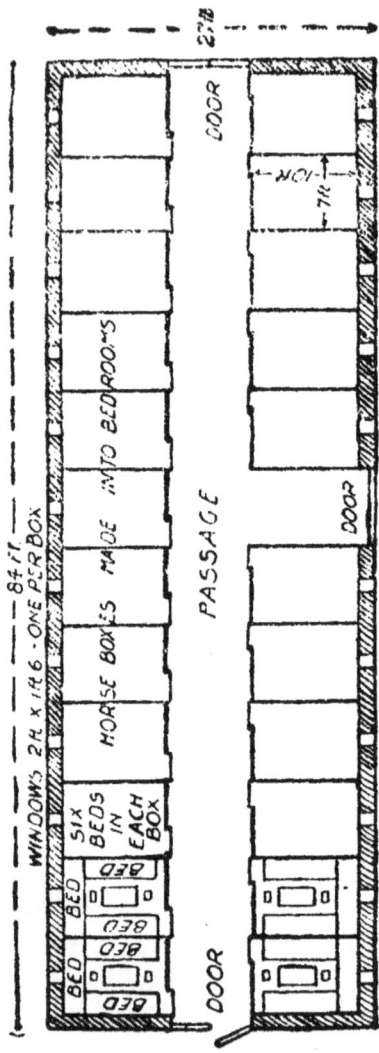

PLAN OF GROUND FLOOR

"The ground floor is divided off into twenty-three boxes, each of which contains six bunks in two tiers. Here also a sack of straw is provided for a mattress and the sole bedding is one thin blanket. Six prisoners are housed in each box, and there are also several iron chairs, such as one sees in the London parks, and a small table." — "Impressions of a Neutral," "Daily Mail," June 3rd, 1915.

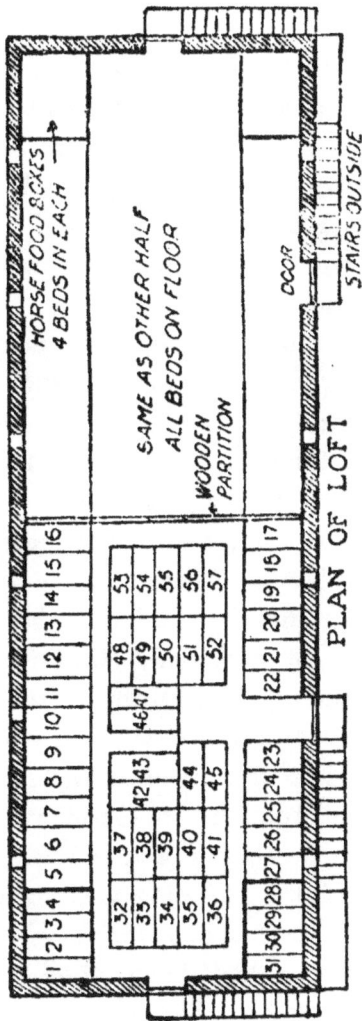

PLAN OF LOFT

HORSE FOOD BOXES
4 BEDS IN EACH →

SAME AS OTHER HALF
ALL BEDS ON FLOOR

← WOODEN
PARTITION

DOOR

STAIRS OUTSIDE

Reproduced by permission from the "Daily Mail."

"Each hut contains two floors. On the upper floor or loft are about a hundred beds, consisting of sacks of straw laid on the floor, with one very thin blanket to each, which may be supplemented by blankets and sheets belonging to the prisoner. These beds are laid side by side as in the diagram." — "Impressions of a Neutral," "Daily Mail," June 3rd, 1915.

amounting in the end to four thousand, were dumped down almost as destitute of food and clothing as if they had been shipwrecked. Had they been shipwrecked, there were six hundred—some say double the number—of merchant sailors there, who might have been more useful than they are now.

These unfortunate individuals were made captives before the war began while they were on board their ships, lying in such places as Hamburg and Bremen. Since the Germans knew that they were going to war, they determined to deprive Great Britain in advance of these possible recruits for her Navy. Many of them were boys from fifteen to eighteen, who had to be given an egg and a glass of milk daily (paid for by the British Government), in addition to the Spartan fare of Ruhleben, to keep them alive.

When the prisoners arrived at the racecourse, with a certain number of Germans, officers, non-commissioned officers and soldiers, and a Commandant and an Acting-Commandant to guard them, chaos reigned for a while, since practically nothing had been done for their reception. The stables had the dung still in them from their last occupation by horses, and the stables played a great part in the play, for those stables and the lofts over them constituted the barracks in which the prisoners were to live.

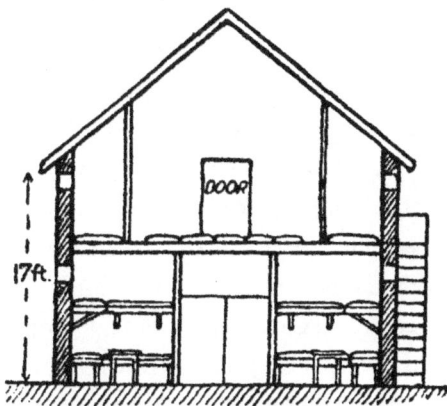

SECTION THROUGH BUILDING

Reproduced by permission from the " Daily Mail."

Transverse section of a Ruhleben barrack. The upper half shows the loft containing about a hundred beds; the lower half shows two horse-boxes containing six beds each arranged in two tiers.

Each horse-box had six berths put into it in two tiers, and in each loft about a hundred sacks of straw were laid out side by side and christened beds.

On these the prisoners were made to lie at night, the only bed-cloth provided by the

German Government being a blanket as thin as a tablecloth, though prisoners were allowed to provide other blankets and sheets of their own as soon as they could get them, if they had the means to buy them or could become provided with them by friends. Most of them slept in their overcoats and all their other clothes, except their boots and their collars. Their beds were so close to each other that when anyone turned in his sleep he woke somebody else, and they were only allowed to sleep until six in the morning, when the sentry came round and called out " Aufstehen ! " (Get up !) and they had to get up and troop away two hundred yards in the cold and the darkness to washing-sheds, which had less than one tap to a hundred persons, no hot water and no protection from draughts.

The people in the horse-boxes, when they got rid of the smell of the filth and the smell of their predecessors, the horses, were rather better off, for their six bunks were arranged in two tiers round three sides of the box, which had a table and iron garden chairs and the luggage of its occupants in the middle. They did not wake each other when they turned in the night. There were twenty-three of these boxes on the ground floor of each barrack.

The food was on a par with the sleeping accommodation. They did not get any until two hours and a half after they had been awakened, but they were allowed to promenade outside until breakfast was ready. Breakfast, as Francis Gribble has told us, consisted " of dry bread and coffee; and the bread was such as the poorest of the poor in England would refuse with scorn, while the alleged coffee was merely a decoction of acorns, with a little sugar in it, but no milk."

At half-past nine the occupants of each hut were lined up under their guards and taken to the kitchen to fetch their loaves of bread when it was their day to get bread, for they received three days' dole at a time.

Then they promenaded again until twelve o'clock, when they had to line up once more for the distribution of their dinner, which consisted of soup only.

After dinner, until half-past three, when the prisoners were given their letters, if there were any for them, they walked about the camp, and smoked or went to their sacks and slept.

179   12*

At five-thirty acorn-coffee or very poor and watery tea was served to them, with dry bread —not, Dr. Taylor states, " the war-bread served in German beer-restaurants, but a bread specially baked for prisoners of war, and composed of potato-flour, bran, fine sawdust, and even thin wisps of straw." The neutral who wrote the report in " The Daily Mail " saw bread of a different type, made of potato-flour and quite black. When served out it was very dry, and though it had to last three days, weighed only four ounces over the pound.

The soup was of a very inferior quality and generally very badly cooked, as the condition of the vegetables in it showed. For weeks at a time no meat was ever supplied. The sausages served out instead of coffee at five-thirty were never eaten by those who had private supplies of food.

They had no place to eat their meals in except the room in which they slept. They had to take their bowls and form in queues outside the grand-stand or tea-house kitchen* (according to the barrack they were in). The distribution of food for each meal took two hours.

* See plan page 41.

The Conditions of Ruhleben Camp

At eight forty-five the guards ordered the prisoners to retire to their beds, and at nine o'clock lights were put out and no more talking was allowed.

In the early days of the camp the prisoners were only allowed to play games like chess between supper and bed-time; cards were strictly forbidden—just as games like cricket and football were forbidden in the day-time. Later on all games were allowed, if there was no playing for money.

"In the early days of November, 1914," says No. VIII. of "In Ruhleben Camp," "when the about four thousand inhabitants of this camp were collected and sent here, and were placed indiscriminately in the various barracks without any idea of what to do or where to go, it became apparent at once that some sort of civil organization was necessary to assist the military authorities in getting the camp into working order, and also to make it as bearable as possible for the prisoners themselves. Each barrack, therefore, elected a captain to act as its spokesman, and as intermediary between the barrack and the military authorities. Each captain then nominated in his barrack a vice-captain, and also appointed a captain for each loft, two postmen and a cashier; and as occasion arose, a laundryman, relief officer, policeman, firemen, etc., were added to the list of barrack officials. The fourteen barrack captains elected two of their number as captain and vice-captain of the camp, and as spokesmen between themselves as a body and the military authorities, and from the first held regular daily meetings, at which they received instructions from the authorities, for publication in their respective barracks and in the camp, and also discussed as a body any points of interest or difficulty (and there have been many) arising in individual barracks. They also attended to a large number of details in connection with the general welfare of the camp, not the least of which was the making-up of many and varied barrack-lists and the answering of innumerable questions. At a later date, as any members of their body resigned or were released, the military authorities appointed new captains to take their places. The camp secretary and treasurer has always been considered a captain and has attended and voted at all the meetings from the commencement. With the exception of permission to walk on the race-course before it was opened to the camp in general, and a reserved form at some of the earlier concerts, the captains have had no privileges which were not available to any other member of the camp. They receive no remuneration, and pay just as much as anyone else for goods they buy at the canteens. They are not free agents, and their actions individually or as a body are always subject to the approval of the military authorities.

" The captains are distinguished by a white band round the arm, bearing the inscription, ' Captain No. — Barrack.'

" In the early part of the year, as the work had increased largely, it was decided to extend the organization on the lines of an English municipality, and a scheme was drawn up, and approved by the authorities, by which the following departments were created : finance, education, recreation, kitchens, canteens, sanitation and watch and works. A committee was formed for each department, consisting generally of two captains and three members of the camp, each committee having power to co-opt any members of the camp, who possessed knowledge likely to be of service in their particular department. When the playing fields were opened, the recreation committee was subdivided into Sports Control and Entertainments' Committees."

" Elected " is a comparative term. Whatever the form of election may have been, the captains were indicated, Ruhlebenites tell me, by the military authorities themselves, as men who for various reasons could be trusted with the post—the chief reasons being that they were *personæ gratæ* to the authorities, and likely to be possessed of enough influence to carry out orders. Some of them, at any rate, were pro-Germans, though others were excellent fellows. It was because they had been indicated in this way that they ventured to defy public opinion and oppose a representative Entertainments' Committee for so long. The pages of the journal which was published in Ruhleben, under the title of " In Ruhleben Camp," are full of indignation at the arbitrary conduct of the Entertainments' Committee, especially in the matter of taking possession of all funds which were earned by the entertainments, and spending them as they thought fit for any camp purpose, without letting the unfortunates whose exertions had made the money see any accounts.

The first committee which was formed to represent the prisoners was disbanded by the authorities. But eventually, late in 1915, four places on the Entertainments' Committee (of ten members including the chairman) were given to genuine representatives of the prisoners.

That was Ruhleben's Civil Government. Its Military Government consisted at first (not counting Count Schwerin, who ranked above the commandant) of a commandant, a staff of officers and about three dozen guards, who were distributed two or three to each barrack, distinguished by a black, white and red band on the arm, bearing the number of the barrack to which they were attached.

In September, 1915, when a measure of Home Rule was accorded to the camp, these soldiers were removed from the barracks, to the unconcealed satisfaction of their inmates, and, gradually increased to about two hundred, patrolled in shifts round the walls and fences.

The commandant was Baron von Taube, described to me by a very impartial and clear-minded man who was imprisoned in Ruhleben for the best part of a year, as a decentish sort of fellow, who was afraid of being hauled over the coals if he was caught being humane. He had his wife with him.

" The other officials," says Mr. A. D. McLaren, " behaved like Prussians, often brutal, but never what we should call humane."

During the early months of Ruhleben, Mr. Israel Cohen tells us : " Almost all the barrack-guards were strict and occasionally savage, and showed scant ceremony in dragging us out of bed at six-thirty, if we were still between our sheets when they pulled our doors open ; but in the course of time they were tamed. The cases of brutality occurred almost all during the first winter. One of the worst was the battering and bruising of a poor Maltese lad, without provocation, by a cowardly soldier ; though much worse was the case of a sailor who was so badly bruised in his cell by a couple of guards, that he had to be removed to the camp hospital, where he died. On one occasion a prisoner

in Barrack VII., while washing early in the
morning in the passage, was violently assaulted
by a soldier, who was punished by being trans-
ferred from the easy job of barrack-guard to the
much more arduous one of sentry. There was
a certain ' Feldwebel ' Meyer, who was notorious
for his cruelty, and who, one summer night,
out of pure malignity, threw a lot of prisoners'
underclothing that was hanging on a line into
a dustbin, and pitched several deck-chairs into
a trench that was being dug in front of Barrack
VII. He was reported to the Baron for this act
of malevolence, but it was not until he had
been caught drunk and sentenced to a day in
the cells that his prowess was given an opportunity of distinguishing itself at the Front."

The stables and tea-house with which the
camp originally started were in time increased
to twenty-three, but the original number of
captains—fourteen—was not altered, because the
later barracks were considered as annexes of the
barracks whose overflow they received.

The great objection to the lofts was that
though they were ten feet high under the highest
point of the roof, their châlet roofs came down

to within four feet and a half of the floor at the sides, thus reducing the air-space inordinately.

For a meeting-room the prisoners had only the hall formed underneath the tiers of seats of one of the grand-stands, which, being of modern brick and cement construction, sufficed for the purpose. In this hall a stage was erected and a complete theatre installed, with scenery, dressing-rooms, orchestra, etc. The betting-boxes were boarded up to afford small rooms for study, musical practice, etc., and in other parts of this building space was allotted for a carpenter's, a tailor's, a barber's and a cobbler's shops.

Later on part of the place under this grand-stand was cut off for a cinema-hall, to which the entrance-charge was just over a penny.

This roused mixed feelings among the prisoners. On Nov. 1st, 1915, Mr. Gerard, the United States' Ambassador at Berlin, who has taken the part of the prisoners so fearlessly, wrote :

" Besides the space for the stage and the auditorium, there was a large part of the hall which was used as a lumber room for stage property and as a carpenter's shop, and was of no further use. This portion of the hall was cut off and used as a cinema show, the store-room for stage scenery and the carpenter's shop being moved outside the hall. The space occupied for the cinematograph could not in any way be missed by the theatre, and has had the advantage of adding a new means of amusement for the camp. I cannot see how the intro-duction of this cinema show has in the least affected the comfort of the hall."

But the returned prisoner appointed by Sir Edward Grey to comment on the same report of Mr. G. W. Minot, on which Mr. Gerard had based his comment, said :

" One of the three stands (tribunes) has a hall underneath, and this is used for every con-ceivable purpose. In August a considerable portion of it has been cut off for a cinema-show, and this loss of space has largely affected the comfort in the hall—or perhaps it is better to say, has greatly increased the discomfort there."

One would like to hear the comment of the

unæsthetic minority of the Ruhleben prisoners, who were constantly complaining that the only place where they could get some light and some warmth—namely, the hall under the grand-stand—was taken up every night by some society or some committee, or some performance for which the entrance-fee was too large for their pockets. When it is remembered that however much money your relatives sent you, you were not allowed more than ten shillings a week pocket-money, and that the majority of the inhabitants had only five shillings a week pocket-money, there was something to be said for their protest, though a stall at " The Frivolity Theatre," Ruhleben, only costs you ninepence, and a circle sixpence. This section of humanity used openly to say that it only went to Debates because they were free, although I suppose there was no charge for the Church of England services, which took place on Wednes-day evenings after the First of September. But smoking would, of course, not be permitted at the services.

There is a very great deal in the magazine about smoking. Nobody ever seems to have been too poor for that—just as when bicycles were the rage in England, nobody was too poor to have a ten-guinea bicycle; there were usually as many bicycles in the house as you kept servants, even if the family could not afford them; but bicycles laughed at love, just as love laughs at locksmiths, and they went the way of all the earth. To return to Ruhleben—" the great difficulty about the debates," said a returned prisoner to me, " was the want of lighting. Not that debates require an extraordinary amount, unless you are going to read your speech. Sometimes," he said, " we had a candle or two to improve matters."

Seriously speaking, the want of light was the greatest of all the hardships with which the prisoners had to contend at Ruhleben, though they were supposed to have electric-light, in which Germany aspired to lead the world. The poor people who were sent to bed at a quarter to nine and had their lights and their conversation extinguished at nine, had no light to get to bed by, except the glimmer of the electric will-o'-the-wisp round the corner in the passage. There was, therefore, a competition for the top berths in the boxes nearest the light, so that, as a humorist observed, " you could swot Russian in bed."

Now, after many months of agitating, prisoners are allowed to have candles in their boxes if they are enclosed in safety-lamps—which was certainly an indispensable precaution in wooden barracks, when people lay on sacks of straw, and later of wood-fibre.

These equivalents for beds were never properly appreciated until the sheep—meaning the German " British "—were separated from the goats, and put into two or three barracks by themselves, when the order went forth that no straw-sacks might be removed from the barracks which were going to be occupied by the sheep, but that the sheep might bring their own straw-sacks from the barracks where they were, the result being that the goats had to do without beds until they could afford to buy them and were able to do so. But the goats were glad to get rid of the sheep, even on those terms, because they were able for the future to say what they liked about Ruhleben without being reported to the flighty Taube.

The really worst feature of the lighting, from the health point of view, was that the barrack-lofts, in which half the prisoners lived, were so dimly lit by day that, in the opinion of the American Ambassador, their occupants, being compelled to spend a good deal of their time there, were likely to have their eyesight permanently injured. One riotous recalcitrant of fifty was given seventy-two hours in the cells for making a skylight in the roof of a hayloft, because " although he pleaded the necessity of ventilating and illuminating the dark hole in which he dwelt, he was declared guilty of damaging military property."

" The prisoners, before entering the cells," says Mr. Israel Cohen, " were temporarily deprived of the contents of their pockets and of their braces. The cells were in Barrack XI., as this was already occupied in September, 1914; they comprised two horse-boxes, each divided by a wooden partition into two cells, which were furnished merely with a wooden plank for a bed. There the offenders, equipped solely with their blankets and bowl, with a ration of black ' war bread ' and cold water each day, ruminated and repented. After completing their sentence the prisoners had to sweep out their cells with a broom, and they then received their belongings —and their braces—back again."

During the wet weather the new wooden sheds, especially Nos. 16, 17, 18, 19 and, to some extent 13, which was built towards the end of 1914 and mainly occupied by negroes, were, in the language of the American Embassy, difficult of entry and exit, owing to the water which then practically surrounded them. And in spite of the water-proof roofs of the new wooden sheds, the rain found its way in. And none of them had any accommodation for washing except No. 19, and when the winter came on it was not pleasant to contemplate having to walk in some cases over two hundred yards, to three wash-houses which had to serve the occupants of ten barracks ; nor would they be pleasant for waiting your turn, since they were very draughty and had, of course, neither heating nor hot water.

No. 19 was the " Schonungsbaracke " (a sort of hospital), where up to ten ailing prisoners were kept under observation in the *Revierstube* (ward), and in the adjoining room there were fifteen pairs of beds, in twos, one above the other, assigned to convalescent or delicate persons. This was the only barrack which had a W.C. in it, and it had only one, reserved for the use of the patients in the *Revierstube*. The pampered individuals in the *Revierstube* had seaweed mattresses, and sheets and pillows, and they and the convalescent people were provided with more suitable food, owing to the exertions of Mr. Stanley Lambert. But the camp authorities did not provide them; the captains had to do that from camp and relief funds.

The Casino is not, as some English people have supposed, the camp infirmary; it is the mess-room of the non-commissioned officers and the men. Special permits are granted to those prisoners who require better food than the camp-menu supplies, and can afford to pay for it, to use it; they can have beer with their food there.

Invalids who need still greater care are sent to Dr. Weiler's sanatorium in Berlin (Nussbaum Allee, 38, Charlottenburg). Mr. Minot, the representative of the American Ambassador who visited it, reported:

" This sanatorium has two divisions, one where

7 marks per day per person is paid, and the
other where 10 marks per day is paid. The
men who are unable to pay for their treatment
are provided with the less expensive treatment
free, the expenditure being disbursed from the
British funds held at this Embassy, while those
men who have sufficient money may, if they
choose, pay themselves for the more expensive
class of housing. The rooms are all very clean
and well-lighted, and the beds seem to be clean
and comfortable. In the less expensive division
there are five or six beds in a room, but the rooms
are large, and there is no hardship entailed in
this concentration. The patients have a small
yard for exercise, with one or two trees in it,
but their chief complaint is that it is impossible
for them to have the same freedom as in the
camp at Ruhleben. The 10-mark patients have
a much larger and more attractive garden of at
least two acres in which to walk, and there are
only two in each room. The patients are all
given five meals a day, consisting of a first and
second breakfast, dinner, tea and supper. These
meals are not very large, but they certainly afford
sufficient nourishment to men who are supposedly

invalids. The patients say that the quality of the food is excellent."

Mr. Stanley Grimm, who was himself a patient at the Weiler Sanatorium, does not agree with Mr. Minot's report. He says that first-class patients now pay sixteen to eighteen marks a day; that they are very lucky if they get into rooms with only two beds; that the food is certainly not sufficient in quantity, and that the patients do not consider the food of excellent quality, though they may have said so to Mr. Minot to avoid getting into trouble. If a patient in the lower division complained he was told that he must go into the higher division or go back to Ruhleben. Mr. Grimm considered Weiler's Sanatorium a purely money-making concern, where they gave you bad value for your money, but were kind. Mr. Grimm says that the patients at the Schonungsbaracke are under a great debt to Mr. Lambert.

The dentist and the oculist who waited on the camp drew much stronger expressions of opinion from the commentator in the British White Paper on Mr. G. W. Minot's report to Mr. Gerard. He said of the dentist:

"This man has spoiled the natural and artificial teeth of many prisoners in the camp and has charged outrageously high fees for doing so. Two prisoners of the camp now practise there and have a perfectly and lavishly equipped place for the purpose; the fitting-up of this place is reputed to have cost several thousand marks."

Of the oculist he speaks with even greater severity :

"I have not come across a single one of his patients who speaks well of him. It was the unanimous opinion of all that he dragged his cases on indefinitely. There has been much correspondence about him between his patients and the American Embassy. When he first came to the camp, Mr. Lambert, who also acts as interpreter for the doctor, arranged with him that the fees should be 5 marks for the first visit and 3 marks for every subsequent one. Very soon after this the captains or Embassy fund increased fees to 10 marks and 5 marks respectively. It is not for me to express any opinion upon this rather high scale of payment, but I feel convinced that there are few specialists, if any, in Germany now who earn so rich a harvest as Dr. Halben does from prisoners of war who are fortunate to have the British Relief Fund behind them."

I now come to the all-important question of food. The camp allowance for each prisoner at Ruhleben, as reported by Dr. Alonzo Engelhart Taylor, the American food expert sent by the Ambassador of the United States to Ruhleben, dated May 4th, 1916, was, for each man per week : Seven ounces of fresh meat, including bones, fat and gristle ; fresh fish, about seven and a half ounces (or seven ounces of sausage or " légumes ") ; the potato ration was about nine pounds per week. The bread ration is not given, but non-working military prisoners get about four pounds and three-quarters. Many of the civil prisoners received little or substantially nothing from the outside, as can be argued from the fact of Jews appearing at the camp kitchen to secure food which was to them not ritualistically clean. Dr. Taylor says that the reduction in allotment of food supplies at Ruhleben was made all the more striking by the fact that the military prisoners of war, as a group, received at the time he wrote as much or more food units per man as the civil prisoners at Ruhleben received.

A returned Ruhlebenite told me that the food question would have been much more aggravated but for the fact that those who had sufficient parcels from home, or were able to buy it, did not eat the camp food at all; and that this made it sufficient for those who received no help from home, because the amount *issued* for the camp was calculated for the whole four thousand prisoners, whether they took it or not, while it was *divided* between those who did desire it. In other words, a proportion—say five-eighths of the prisoners—divided between them the food intended for the whole.

The meat contractor appears to have been an absolute rogue, who sent nearly all gristle, bone and fat for the pitiful seven ounces per week allowed to each prisoner.

The report of the correspondent of " The Manchester Guardian," July 3rd, 1916, said :

" The shortage of meat has necessitated the finding of some substitutes. Once upon a time liver sausage and blood sausage were given in place of meat, but these have become now almost as rare and precious as meat itself, and hence the product known as *Kriegswurst*, or war-sausage, is now served. This is made of blood-soaked bread and melted fat ; each man is given a slice about four inches by three, but the stuff is so soft and flabby that he has to eat it with a spoon, if he can eat it at all. Butter, margarine and condensed milk have not been sold at the camp canteen for the last seven months ; sugar is brought into camp only once a month, and cheese, the poorest quality at two shillings a pound, has become scarce."

Mr. Gribble says that the fraudulent contractor promised them for Christmas Day some of the meat which they ought to have received every day. His portion consisted of raw fat bacon, which he had no means of cooking, so he threw it away. The lucky ones received a small slice of coarse corned beef. But the raw bacon may have been offered to him genuinely, because the country Germans consider raw bacon with brown bread a delicacy. My personal feelings would have been the same as Mr. Gribble's at receiving that for my only meat of the year.

These, roughly speaking, are the crude conditions of Ruhleben. I shall proceed in the next chapter to show what the indomitable British spirit effected in the way of solacing its captivity, instead of sitting down by the waters of Babylon (Ruhleben is on the Spree) and weeping. In the finest " Admirable Crichton " vein, they set to work to shorten the days of their captivity with a wonderful system of classes—a sort of University of Utopia—and the introduction of the wild sports of their native land, such as league football matches between the various barracks, league cricket matches, reminding one of the House challenge cups at our Public-Schools, a tennis tournament (for which there were two hundred and forty entries made by one hundred players), a golf tournament (for the ten interned professionals, at any rate), hockey, and a little boxing in a shed, which they called " Wonderland." Theatrical and musical entertainments were naturally legion, and there was a very flourishing Debating Society, at which subjects of any interest to the camp were of course debarred.

CHAPTER VII

" THE UNIVERSITY OF RUHLEBEN "

(The Famous System of Classes established in
the Camp)

I HAVE already alluded to these classes as
the University of Utopia. They strike
me as one of the most wonderful and splendid
achievements of which I have ever heard.
That in a body of 4,500 British men, suddenly,
through no fault of their own, interned in
an enemy country, the majority should settle
down with a fixed resolve to leave the place far
better educated than when they entered it, by
acquiring modern languages, or knowledge of
some science or the like, or even dead languages,
strikes me as the finest way of finding a blessing
in the disguise of a colossal misfortune.

Perhaps the most extraordinary and the most

solidly useful species of education confered at Ruhleben is that of enabling merchant-sailors to acquire all the knowledge which is necessary for passing the examinations for Mate's and Master's certificates. As there are, variously estimated, from six hundred to double the number of merchant-sailors interned at Ruhleben, this is a priceless educational boon.

As good luck would have it, a great many teachers are interned at Ruhleben ; teachers, like professional musicians, incline to Germany for a summer holiday, because of the prospect of increasing their professional knowledge. And there were also, of course, a large number of men, mostly youngish, engaged in teaching English in Germany, when the war broke out.

The staff of the hundred classes of the Ruhleben Camp consists chiefly of University men, or men whose profession is teaching.

Who knows if this impromptu university, which has arisen at Ruhleben, may not lead to a Ruhleben method of teaching ?—a method of imparting all kinds of knowledge, based on a commonsense and practical system, which has been evolved by able and sympathetic teachers for imparting knowledge personally, in the absence of many of the aids to education which are ordinarily used. Books must be a difficulty in such a place, though their entry is permitted and they are sold at the proper price.*

The books directly used are bought, but there must be a shortage of the side-aids to acquiring a knowledge of the subject, in the shape of the number of books which we are apt to use in studying any one book. Take, for example, the classics : To study your Herodotus or your Virgil, you do not only use a Greek Lexicon and a Latin Dictionary; you want Dictionaries of Greek and Latin Geography, of Classical Biography and Mythology, of Classical Antiquities, and particular books by great scholars who have made studies of these authors. You would have to do with a great deal less in Ruhleben ; even if you did not have to go back to the methods of thirteenth-century Paris and Oxford. These are

* The following advertisement appears in No. 2 of the Camp Journal :

" Books, music and war-maps at net shop prices, supplied at shortest possible notice—no extra charge, not even for postage. Apply between 2 and 4 p.m. to F. L. Mussett, Barrack V., Box 22."

the methods pursued to-day at El-Azhar, the great University of Islam in Cairo, where an Ulema stands against a column of the Mosque, which serves to mark the place where his scholars will find him. He has always a blackboard, on which he can write or draw to drive a point home, and very often that is the only appliance for learning visible, except the tablets or note-books of the students. I expect that there is a good deal of teaching of that kind at Ruhleben, as well as of uncommonly close study of books by the students, to while away the long hours of their imprisonment. If there is as much of this teaching as I imagine there must be, I am sure that its efficacy will be demonstrated, and it might well lead to a " Ruhleben System of Teaching."

The lecture, of course, appertains at Oxford, but unless the lecturer is recognized as very expert in making a lecture an engine of teaching, lectures are openly despised there and are attended with reluctance, as taking you away, for so much precious time, from the study of books on which your class in the Honour List depends.

The great difficulty in the way of the hundred classe s of Ruhleben has from the very beginning lain in the paucity of accommodation, which is relieved to some extent in summer, by having classes of all sorts on the actual grand-stands from which fashionable Berlin used to watch English jockeys dividing the prizes of its classic races.

Incidentally, I wondered what had become of these jockeys. Had they been repatriated, out of the gratitude and under the influence of their Imperial and princely patrons, as benefactors of Deutschland—if not of Deutschtum ? If not, what had become of them ? They could not have been still interned at Ruhleben, or we should have heard of classes in which jockeys, sitting on dummy steeds, made of trunks of trees, taught aspirants to Turf honours to ride races on phantom horses, just as the merchant-seamen are learning how to be mates and masters on phantom ships. Mr. Hughes, the writer in the " Cornhill Magazine," supplied the answer. " After a few days certain high officers in the Army, whose racing establishments were spoiling by neglect, obtained the release of a number of jockeys and trainers, to the lively scandal of the public."

Remarking to a Ruhlebenite that a grand-stand appeared to me a difficult place to convert into an open-air class-room, because its seats would not have desks in front of them and its tiers would be too narrow to accommodate tables, he said that this was not so; that the tiers were wide enough for a student to have a little table in front of him—students, it appears, are as apt to have portable tables as the Mrs. Grundy of the Victorian Era was apt to have a camp-stool to rest on while she was performing her duties against Society. A certain class of student, he said, instead of bringing a table, brought a deck-chair, where he lay in the attitude of the man on the steamer studying the elements. The picture he drew of these Berlin grand-stands, with their broad tiers, suggested to me that either the provision of accommodation for portly persons must be a serious question for the proprietors of German race-courses, or else that the German wants to " go one better " in grand-stands, like everything else, and insists on having Pullman grand-stands, where the efforts of the toiling British jockey may be watched from arm-chairs.

" The University of Ruhleben "

In any case, for a long time the Third Grand-Stand of the Ruhleben race-course was learning's most valuable handmaid, though no one was allowed on it between 8 p.m. and 8 a.m.—on pain of endangering the whole of the teaching facilities extended to the prisoners.

The effect of the want of accommodation on the chances of learning is worth while tracing in some detail. It must be borne in mind that there are two great teaching influences at Ruhleben—the Camp School and the Arts and Science Union, which work in with each other, having agreed that teaching shall be left to the School and lectures and education circles to the Union.*

* For their temporary disagreement see letter of August 28th, 1916, page 168.

" The two educational bodies in the camp, the Camp School and the Arts and Science Union, had had a quarrel, which finally burst into flame at the school-teachers' meeting on the 5th of this month. The atmosphere became so heated and there seemed to be so little chance of an adjustment at the meeting that an advisory committee was formed, to whom the two respective committees might refer their difficulties. Masterman refused to be a member, and those elected were Prichard, Mackenzie and Andrews. . . . So salutary was the mere existence of this committee that most of the difficulties, and certainly the acute ones, were got over in a week."

In Ruhleben

On July 26th, 1915, a general meeting of nearly a hundred teachers of the Camp School was held in the loft of Barrack 6, which was at that time set aside for educational uses, to hear the report of the School Committee, which had set a fine example of patriotism by announcing its decision to retire, in order that its place might be taken by a more efficient committee.

From that report we learn that in the early days of January, 1915, Mr. Reynolds, at the suggestion of the Arts and Science Union, called a meeting of teachers, with the object of setting up a school in the camp. A committee was then elected to undertake this work, of which Mr. Ford became the chairman, and Mr. Reynolds the secretary. " Two possible courses were open to the Committee—(1) to find out what the camp could teach, and offer a syllabus based on that inquiry; (2) to find out what the camp wanted to learn, and to satisfy that demand as well as possible. The second course was adopted, and a suggestive syllabus was drawn up and circulated, together with application forms. Over eleven hundred of these were returned, applying in most cases for three classes (the maximum offered to each), and ranging over a very wide field of subjects, nearly all of which, however, the Committee had reasonable hopes of being able to satisfy.

" Though the demand for instruction was thus shown to be very strong, the committee now met their first disappointment ; for the Arts and Science Union, who had undertaken the responsibility of finding accommodation for class-teaching, were quite unable to do anything in this matter. All sorts of suggestions were made in the proper quarters, but nothing came of them, and the school's effort thus early received a check from which it has never fully recovered. And even now the question of accommodation cannot be considered altogether satisfactory. In order, however, to prevent waste of time and disappointment of intending pupils, and in order to show how strong and real was the demand for education, the committee now proposed to start a system of classes in boxes and loft corners, for which purpose a sub-committee was appointed.

" This sub-committee then circulated slips,

asking for the use of boxes and loft-corners, and therein formed some thirty classes, consisting for the most part of the occupants of those places and their acquaintances. Feeling, however, that this system was rapidly exhausting the teaching capacity of the camp, and leading to an unsatisfactory grouping of pupils—difficult to re-group on a sound basis when proper accommodation could be found—the sub-committee refrained from pressing this development, forming classes only where exceptional keenness was shown. With the advent of warm weather, and the possibility of class-teaching being undertaken on the Third Grand-Stand, and later in the loft of Barrack 6, the activity of the school developed rapidly, until on July 24th, 1915, some seventy-five classes were at work, giving tuition to some seven hundred pupils."

The committee originally proposed to invite a voluntary subscription from pupils, or from others interested in promoting the school's welfare, but they felt that the uncertainty of the continuation of the classes did not justify them in asking for these subscriptions. Moreover, when the Camp Education Committee came into existence, the school came within the captains' scheme for that committee's activities, so that it could look to the committee to defray its expenses, as it had expressed the wish that instruction in the Camp Schools should as far as possible be free. The only financial help actually given was a renewable credit of fifty marks for petty expenses, advanced by the Education Committee.

The total expenditure of the school, up to July 24th, 1915, was 294 marks, 95 pfennigs, a little under £15. The total income was 18 marks, leaving a deficit of 276 marks, 95 pfennigs. As arranged, the accounts showing to whom the school was in debt were presented in a balance-sheet to the Education Committee.

The classes formed by Mr. Wimpfheimer, at one time numbering thirty-three, with nearly two hundred pupils, had been united with the School some weeks before the resignation of that patriotic committee, Mr. Wimpfheimer becoming a member of the School Committee.

In conclusion, the Camp School Committee

said quite truly : " We have called into being a competent and energetic body of teachers, from whom can now be elected a new representative committee that will be wholly capable, in light of the pioneer committee's experience, to carry on the administration of the Camp School with every reasonable hope of solid success."

At the general meeting of the hundred teachers on Saturday, July 26th, 1915, the old committee's scheme of re-organization, recommended on the occasion of their retirement, was, with little amendment, adopted. The scheme divided the school into nine departments, based on the classes already in existence and those desirable and likely to be formed in the immediate future—viz., (1) French, (2) English and German, (3) Spanish, including Italian, Russian and Dutch, (4) Science and Mathematics, (5) Engineering, (6) Nautical, (7) Handicrafts, (8) Commercial, (9) Arts. Each department was given a member of committee to represent it, and to these were added a chairman, a treasurer and the School Requisites' manager, who, in addition to being members of the General

Committee, formed an executive sub-committee, which met every day from 3 to 4.30 p.m., in the School Office—a shed between Barracks 2 and 3.

The result of the reconstitution from within was soon visible. By September there were fifteen hundred students and a hundred teachers, most of them University men, or men who were teachers by profession. The Education Committee showed its recognition of the work which had been done by appointing three members of the School Committee to its own board, and arranging for several hundred volumes to be sent out from England for a Reference Library. The two great problems still to be considered were the question of funds needed by the organization and the question of accommodation for classes when the cold weather came on. Easier to settle were the questions of holding examinations and keeping full class registers.

To give its students places for study, the Camp School Committee appealed to the Summer House Club Committee to allow students to study in the card-rooms where members played cards—presumably as a nice quiet place.

The Arts and Science Union had already invited any member of the camp who wished to have the use of the cubby-holes under the grand-stand to apply to its Allocation Secretary —each student to be allowed the use of a cubby-hole for two hours a day. Students were warned not to fail in making applications while the question of obtaining space for study was again under discussion.*

With respect to funds, the school decided to issue this appeal to the camp :

* In 1916 the facilities for studying comfortably, conveniently and quietly became much increased by the opening of the Y. M. C. A. building.

From letter of January 16th, 1916.

" During the holidays the Y. M. C. A. Hall has been completed, so that there is now a large, well-lighted room, where many can read in quiet and freedom from smoke. The reference-library and several small class-rooms are attached to the big hall, which can hold about four hundred and fifty."

" RUHLEBEN CAMP SCHOOL

" To the Camp !

" Appeal for Funds.

" The success that has been the happy result of the school's efforts has led naturally to an increase in expenditure. Up till now this has been met by special grants, and while the current expenditure will continue to be met in this way, the very considerable initial expense for equipment—partitioning, books and apparatus—is one which the committee feel might well be borne in part by those who benefit from the school.

" Like practically all other activities in the camp, the school is essentially a voluntary service ; but when in these days of general sacrifice so much money from within the camp is spent on amusement the committee feel that this appeal for a voluntary subscription for education will surely meet with a generous response.

" Subscriptions should be handed into the

School Office (between Bar. 2 and 3) during office hours 3—4.30 any afternoon, when a receipt will be given."

*   *   *   *   *

" The educational work of the camp is suited in the main to meet the requirements of three classes of individuals : 1. Those whose internment here has interrupted their preparations for such examinations as the London Matriculation, the various University Degrees or the Board of Trade nautical examinations. 2. Those who have already entered upon a commercial or professional career. 3. Those who pursue some form of learning for Learning's sake."

It is natural at this point to pass to the autumn announcement made in 1915 by the Arts and Science Union, which not only did so much for Education, but also for the social life of the prisoners.

" The University of Ruhleben "

" Arts and Science Union

" Early in the year the A. and S. U. had
organized open-air teaching on the Third Grand-
Stand at a time when the work of the school,
an off-shoot of the Union, had come to a stand-
still for want of space. As the weather grew
warmer, the school followed suit in making use
of the Third Grand-Stand and a re-organization
of its administration took place. Class-teaching
being outside the original plan of the Union, it
was agreed recently between the committees
of the School and the Union to turn over the
whole of the Union's lectures and classes to the
control of the School, certain members of the
Union being at the same time added to the
School Committee. This agreement was
accepted by a general meeting of the Union on
September 4th.

" The circles appointed representatives who
met on September 11th, to consider what
should be their relationship to the other educational bodies in the camp. They decided to
regard themselves in future, as in most cases in

219

the past, as part of the Arts and Science Union, and to be represented by that body on the Education Committee."

The Arts and Science Union started its work with a system of lectures (whose time-table is given page 227), on such subjects as mathematics, chemistry, biology, electricity, physics, heredity, and various subjects of ancient and modern literature. In addition to them it arranged for a popular lecture on some technical subject every Wednesday and Saturday at ten, among the first subjects treated being: Fuel Economy, Fire Prevention, The Production of Iron, Producing, Buying and Selling Electricity, Mechanical Flight and The Modern Newspaper. Every Saturday at three there was a popular lecture on some British Colony or foreign country, beginning with Canada, China and Russia.

In addition to this there were Monday evenings in the hall, devoted to artistic work of all kinds, such as an English Folk-Act evening, a lecture on Modern Drama illustrated by short scenes from plays, acted in costume ; a Madrigal

Concert ; a Chamber-Music evening ; a Poetry evening, and so on ; and a weekly meeting of Biologists, Chemists and Physicists on Wednesdays at 6 p.m., to hear papers on subjects of mutual interest, to be followed by a discussion.

Membership of the Union is open to all members of the camp who are in sympathy with its aims ; there is no subscription and all lectures are free to all.

In the August number of the magazine a new series of lectures were announced, on : The Development of England as a Great Power ; The Dynamics of a Particle ; Technical Electro-Chemistry, and Contemporary Composers. At the same time the Ruhleben Camp School had a Marine-Engineering Class, for " Extra Chief's Certificate," where thirty marine-engineers were preparing themselves for this examination ; and practical lectures had been begun on the Diesel Engines, Shorthand and Book-keeping, besides modern languages classes and lectures on such subjects as The History of Philosophy and The Problem of the Freedom of the Human Will. One of the best-attended lectures was that on The Philosophy of Goethe's " Faust."

There was also a large physical drill class, an Indian-club class, and a very largely attended class for the study of Chinese.

The circles of the Arts and Science Union covered a very wide ground. There were French, Italian, Spanish and German Circles; there were Banking, Science, Technical, Social Problems, Nautical and Marine Engineering Circles. " They meet once or twice a week, as the case may be, either to discuss a debatable subject, to listen to a paper read by one of the members, upon which a discussion might follow, or to read a popular work in the language of the circle. The object of these circles is that their meetings should be of an informal character as far as possible. In the Language Circles, for instance, there is a minimum number of members in each circle who speak, read and write the language really well. This gives those who are eager to learn a chance of speaking, and those who are at all nervous a feeling that when speaking they are not addressing a board of examiners.

" The circles have been a huge success. The chief drawback is to find reasonably warm accommodation for their meetings in the winter."

There were, of course, Philistines in the camp, who sneered about everyone wanting to learn several languages at once. " T. G." voiced them, in a witty article, one of the " Phœbe " series.

" We suffer here from a peculiar migrating variety of the genus pupil. I don't know whether it's the climate or not, but you cannot get them to stick to one thing for long. They float round from lecture to lecture, from language to language, and end up as silly as they started. They have come to regard learning the first six chapters of Otto, or the first Berlitz book, as a hobby, a pastime. But further than that you cannot get them to go. I do not suppose there is a single man in the camp who cannot ask you how you feel, how you felt yesterday, in half a dozen different languages, but I doubt if there are more than ten who can say what is wrong with them in three."

The man who supposed " that Norman Angell regards this war as a dirty trick put up by the rest of Europe to undermine his position," said to another man who was at Ruhleben with him,

" We all know that you're having the time of your life here. Stick you down anywhere where you can gas about the Arts and Science Union and addle your brain by learning half a dozen languages at once, and you'd be quite happy. You don't care whether you ever get back to England or not, do you ! "

But the Eisteddfod programme was almost as humorous as the progs of the Philistines, for, in addition to having competitions for choirs of twenty men from each barrack, a vocal quartette, a tenor, bass or baritone solo, a string quartette, 'cello solo, pianoforte solo, wind instrument solo, and conductors to conduct the Camp Orchestra through an unrehearsed piece ; in addition to having a drama and elocution section, an oratory department for the best speech, not more than ten minutes, on " Responsibility," with recitations of a short poem in Italian, Spanish, Russian, German or Welsh, prize essays, poems, etc.——they had *a Fine and Applied Arts' Section, for darning a woollen sock, putting a patch on a piece of provided material, hemming the same and sewing on two buttons, and rope-splicing and knot-tying competitions.*

" The University of Ruhleben "

The Camp School and the Arts and Science Union of Ruhleben are well able to stand a little cheap fun. They will pass into history for certain, as the noblest achievement with which prisoners have ever beguiled a long and painful captivity. Everyone who knows of the work which they have done will sincerely hope that they will do more than that, and find a permanent niche in the educational curriculum of the Country which they have served so well.

The proper way to achieve this is, in my opinion, to have Ruhleben Circles—a Ruhleben Institution of Circles—forming a part of the London University, trying as far as possible to make it a continuation of the work done at Ruhleben by employing as teachers men who taught at Ruhleben. These Ruhleben Circles could supplement the work of existing University Extension and night-classes. Their elastic machinery is exactly suited for giving sort-of-post-graduate courses to adults engaged in all the multifarious professions, trades and services of the workers of London. For the men who were taught in the " Circles " of Ruhleben were adults, some of them fifty years old and more, so

the machinery would be good for enabling pro-
miscuous adults to acquire whatever further
kinds of education they required, by an easy and
natural process of teaching, which, instead of
oppressing them or making them feel small,
made them learn incidentally. There is no
reason why in the time to come the methods of
the Ruhleben University should not be as useful
and famous as Berlitz methods.

" The University of Ruhleben "

TIME-TABLE OF A. & S. U. LECTURES.

Mon.	8–9.	9–10.	10-11.	11-12.	6-7.
	Differential and Integral Calculus, *Bröse.*	German Literature, *Pender* (in German).	Inorganic Chemistry, *Steinberg.*	Alfred de Vigny, *Ford.*	Psychology, *Farmer.*
Tues.	Elementary Biology,*Lechmere.* Radio-activity, *Chadwick.*	English Literature, *Leigh* *Henry.*	Organic Chemistry, *Croad.*	Mechanics, *Bröse.*	Elementary Physics, *Smith.*
Wed.	Electro Chemistry, *Hatfield.*	Heredity, *Pease.*	Euripides, *Coole.*	Electricity and Magnetism, *Chadwick.*	Italian Literature, *Cutayar* (in Italian).
Thurs.	Calculus, *Bröse.*	German Literature, *Pender,* (in German).	Inorganic Chemistry, *Steinberg.*	Alfred de Vigny, *Ford.*	
Fri.	Elementary Biology,*Lechmere.* Radio-activity, *Chadwick.*	English Literature, *Henry.*	Organic Chemistry, *Croad.*	Mechanics, *Bröse.*	Shakespeare, *Ford.*
Sat.	Electro Chemistry, *Hatfield.*	Heredity, *Pease.*	Technical Sugar Chemistry, *Darbishire.* Euripides, *Coole.*	Electricity and Magnetism, *Chadwick.*	Italian Literature, *Cutayar* (in Italian).
Sun.	Elementary Biology,*Lechmere.*	Shakespeare, *Ford.*	Music, *Bainton.*		

Wednesday and Saturday, 2-3, Agricultural Chemistry, *Dickson.* Courses of Lectures on "Colonies and Foreign Countries from the business point of view" and " Popular Technology " will be announced in a few days. The reorganization of the Ruhleben Camp School is being proceeded with.

" WHY ? "

" Thank you, thank you, Captains all,
  Supermen and Buttonmen,
  Deans of Universities.
  Thank you I must
  When I think on that
  Which was,
  Compared to what shall be,
  Or e'en now is,
  Thank you.
  But why ?—why do you do it ?
  Captains all, Supermen and Buttonmen,
  Deans of Universities,
  Why ?
  What is the axe you're grinding ?
  Or is it silly love
  Of mere publicity ?
  Is it vain love of petty power,
  Or the venal gold that sears ?
  Or is it honest love of toil—
  Unselfish thought
  For poor Humanity ? "

From " In Ruhleben Camp."

228

CHAPTER VIII

" THE ADMIRABLE CRICHTON," as played at Ruhleben, was not quite on the lines of Sir J. M. Barrie's farce. For there were fourteen " Admirable Crichtons " there— the fourteen captains, though perhaps the title might have been restricted to the Captain of the Camp, a certain Mr. Powell, who had before the war been manager of a cinema-film business in Berlin, who clothed himself with fairly absolute authority, since he took it on himself not to convey to the board of captains, over which he presided, the various protests addressed to them about the Entertainments' Committee. The Entertainments' Committee was a fearful and wonderful affair, composed of the " eclected " captains. They did not get up entertainments ;

they merely withdrew their opposition to certain entertainments and assumed the expenditure of any money that was made by them. " When I last heard of them," says Mr. A. D. McLaren, " they were still resisting all attempts to make them publish any account of the expenditure of these monies. Very likely they did yield to clamour in the end." I did not come across the account of these Ruhleben profits in any of the journals, Ambassador's confidences and articles of returned Ruhlebenites in our own Press, which I examined.

It must be borne in mind that none of the protests against the Entertainments' Committee, which I have examined, made the slightest insinuation that any member of the Committee had derived any personal advantage from the administration of the profits made by theatrical performances. The complaint was that the people who had made the money by their personal exertions were not allowed to spend the money on preparing further entertainments, or to direct its spending in any way, or even to hear how it had been spent.

It very certainly was not spent in the most

obvious way—the cheapening of the seats, for which such a widespread desire existed, at the theatrical entertainments. Their price, it is true, was only ninepence for stalls, sixpence for dress-circle and threepence for the five rows of pit; but even that is a serious item when your income is five shillings, or at the most ten shillings a week, and you get nothing which you like to eat except what you buy for yourself at the canteen or have sent out from England.

It must also be remembered that there was a large section of the community which did not care for entertainments at all, but cared very much for the hall as a place which was, in a faint, lugubrious way, lighted and heated, where they could sit and smoke. They liked the Debating Society best because it was entirely free, and next to that the Popular Concerts, where the purchase of a penny programme constituted the right of admission. They would have liked their theatre to have cost the same as their cinema—a penny, and used to write letters to the magazine asking the Committee to give them two nights a week without any entertainments.

Truly their Clarksons and their Harkers

displayed such ingenuity in the manufacture of properties that the Ruhleben Dramatic Society deserved all the money which could be made by its productions. Here are some of the secrets of the prison-house, theatrically speaking :

The old armchair, used for every production except " Androcles and the Lion," was made of four sugar-boxes, odd bits of crêpe left over from the curtains and half the shavings from some poor wretch's bed. It did for " Captain Brassbound's Conversion," " The Speckled Band " and " As You Like It," in which, deprived of its back and arms, it was part of a mossy bank. It did for the dainty matrimonial tiffs of the French Players and the gorgeousness of " The Count of Luxemburg." But, to continue using the words of the Ruhleben magazine, " it twice had a bob's-worth of crêpe."

The sofa cost 3 marks, like the rich wooden chair made for Louis XI. of France. With a bit of red crêpe, it was a dining-room sofa ; with green crêpe, it was a drawing-room sofa ; with brown crêpe, it was, as the magazine said, " just the tone for a study." Once it had its back and arms taken off and became a four-poster bed, and for " The Silver Box " it had four nice new legs, made from bits of " Strife " scenery.

Canvas-wood-and-paint English fireplaces cost 7 marks each ; a high club fender, with an up-holstered top, which would not stand sitting on, had for its rails broom-handles bought for two-pence each at the canteen ; it, too, had a crêpe top. In fact, the cheerful widowerhood of Ruhleben was typified by its use of coloured crêpe.

The red crêpe began in the Coliseum scene of " Androcles and the Lion." The green formed the forest in " As You Like It." Ever since those productions all the furniture was covered in red and green crêpe alternately, so that, as the magazine observed, " they never got tired of it."

The curtains were also the wallpaper in a lady's bedroom in " The Speckled Band," and formed the dress of the poet in " The Ballad-Monger."

The flats, which were screens of canvas on light wooden frames, cost 140 marks, but it only cost 6 marks to repaint them for another play.

As to furniture, the furnishing in the study scene of " The Speckled Band," the most elaborate effort at Ruhleben, cost under 40 marks—a couple of sovereigns. The best piece of furniture in the whole repertoire was the little Moorish table, made of the old footlight board. The grandfather clock, made out of two sugar-boxes, with a canvas face, hands cut out of a cigar-box and an ornament on the top of the face taken off a real mirror, cost only 2½ marks.

As to properties, I must quote " In Ruhleben Camp " direct :

" Thinking I might find something interesting, I fished about in the property-box, and my first haul was the roast goose which made me feel so hungry at ' The Ballad-Monger.' Near-to he had hardly as great an effect on me, for one could see he was nothing but sawdust and canvas. The next thing was a rifle. ' Captain Brassbound ' is a long way back, but surely you remember those rifles ?   One broomstick, a bit of webbing, part of a Huntley and Palmer's biscuit-tin for the lock, some paint and hey presto !—there you are, a Lee-Metford guaranteed not to bounce if dropped on the stage, and all for 50 pfennigs. That reminds me ; the carpenters confess to one failure—the poker that behaved so badly in ' The Speckled Band ; ' but then, as they pointed out to me, if Dr. Rylott hadn't dropped it, the beastly thing would never have bounced! At my next dip I got a pair of handcuffs and a revolver ; the former made of bits of wood and rope, and the latter carved out of plaster of Paris, with a pocket-knife. Then came some green bits of cardboard at which the carpenters laughed. They were the leaves of the forest, they explained. It took twenty-five men to cut them out and paint them, and they had a fearful row with the box-office people, who complained that the carpenters had pinched all the cardboard and left them none to make tickets with. ' And the ticket-money was more important than the rotten forest, etc., etc.' "

The footlights at first were candles with condensed-milk tins as shades behind them—a touch quite worthy of " The Admirable Crichton." When the scene had to be changed, they just pulled a string and the lights turned round and shone in your eyes, so that you could not see the scene-shifter's operations in that light ; it was like darkening the theatre at His

Majesty's when the scenes are changed in Shakespeare.

Androcles' lion had a mask made of cloth and paint ; it borrowed somebody's fur gloves for its paws. The lion's head was eventually stolen as a relic.

As to scenery, " Spintho," one of the wits of Ruhleben, wrote :

" When we could not get any scenery at first, we hung curtains round the stage, and told each other that we did not like conventional scenery and that symbolical curtains were much better. I remember one chap, Henry Leigh, I think he called himself, one of those Futurist Johnnies, you know, put on ' As You Like It ' with green curtains and blue music ; no end of a rag it was ! But later on we got regular scenery, and flies and flats and battens and borders, and prosceniums and auditoriums, and what not galore."

Thanks to the inexpensiveness of staging a play,* and the facts that the actors, even the

---

* The only people who were paid were the staff hands, who received between them 30 marks a week. The preparation of the tickets cost 10 marks and the enlarging of the stage in the early days 3.50 marks.

stars, all gave their services for nothing, etc., etc., the Ruhleben Dramatic Society made large sums by some of their plays. "Captain Brassbound's Conversion" made 400 marks (£20), "The Mumming Birds" 900 marks (£45).

To us in our armchairs at home, the selection of plays seems a pretty catholic one. Bernard Shaw's "Captain Brassbound's Conversion," Conan Doyle's "The Speckled Band," W. B. Yeats' "Cathleen Ni Houlihan," Lady Gregory's "Spreading the News" and "The Rising of the Moon" (the last three being productions of the Irish Players at the Abbey Theatre, Dublin), "Don't Laugh," "The Private Secretary," Bernard Shaw's "Androcles and the Lion," Shakespeare's "As You Like It," "The Ballad-Monger," "Scenes from Dickens," "L'Enfant Prodigue," John Galsworthy's "The Silver Box," Bernard Shaw's "Fanny's First Play," Ibsen's "The Master-builders," Oscar Wilde's "The Importance of Being Earnest," R. C. Carton's "Mr. Preedy and the Countess," "Don Juan in Hell," "Strife," a couple of French plays and, last of all, a German play by real actors imported from Berlin. But to some of the 4,500 English in durance vile at Ruhleben it seemed otherwise.

Under the signature " A Corner of Barrack 10," a letter appeared in No. 6 of " In Ruhleben Camp " :

" We read with regret that long-haired devils wish to pump Ibsen, further Shakespeare, etc., into this Lager. We wish those people were anywhere but here ; where box-office receipts would be a more immediate and definite reply from the public than is the case here, where the poor prisoner sighing for ' Charley's Aunt ' would rather bear Elizabethan plays or Ibsen than boredom. Can nothing be done to muzzle these people and prevent them from using our one and only theatre to such vile and pseudo-artistic ends as the production of further pseudo-Shakespeare as badly done as the last ?

" ' Charley's Aunt ' when badly done at least does not offend."

In the same number Mr. Aubrey H. Hersee urges the appointment of a censor of plays, " in order that each play submitted should be carefully read and only passed when considered likely to be of general interest to the camp. There is," said Mr. Hersee, " at present a tendency to produce plays of a lugubrious character, or plays with a purpose ; and as the educational side of the camp is so ably handled by other and more competent authorities, surely the interests of the camp are more studied by using the theatre as a medium of entertainment and amusement ? Such censors should also bear in mind the limitations enforced by our internment, and thus not overtax the leniency shown by a considerate camp."

When full, the ninepenny stalls at Ruhleben Theatre produced 82.50 marks a night ; the sixpenny dress-circle produced 20 marks a night ; five rows of threepenny pit seats produced 30 marks a night. Thus, without the extra rows of pit seats which could be put in, one house was capable of producing 132.50 marks, and two performances paid the cost for most productions. But " As You Like It " was very expensive ; it cost 420 marks ($£21$).

There was a suggestion that the seats should be reduced to threepence-halfpenny and two-pence-halfpenny on the last two nights, but the chairman was afraid that the camp would wait for the cheap nights, and was in favour of reducing the prices every night.

As there were no women allowed in Ruhleben, the female parts had to be taken by men. The pretty girl of the Ruhleben Dramatic Society was a famous Rugby footballer. Fortunately, they had a very good Clarkson, who, with several yards of crêpe, cotton and thread, some old cardboard boxes, a few biscuit-tins and some string and glue, made dresses for one Roman Emperor, two of his courtiers, Christian captives, two female ditto, a few incidental people, a number of gladiators, several soldiers, and a crowd of males, such as an editor, an ox-driver, a slave, a call-boy and a lion—I quote the magazine again.

The theatre was variously alluded to as THE FRIVOLITY and THE ELEPHANT AND CASTLE.

Music was the most serious rival of the drama. They had to form a second musical society because the first refused to recognize Gounod as a classic. The purveyors of music were disposed to be " advanced," like the purveyors of the drama ; it is not surprising that there was a feeling of responsibility in this section, because the interners had made a heavy bag of professional musicians : thirty-six joined the society on the first day.

The first pieces of music which they selected were : Coleridge-Taylor's " Hiawatha's Wedding-Feast," Saint-Saëns' Violin Concerto, Liepunow's Ukraine Rhapsody, Wieniawski's Violin Concerto, and Verdi's Requiem on All Souls' Day, with " The Mikado " at the end, to cheer it up. But they afterwards became more considerate to the audiences, and distributed impartially Bach and Offenbach, Wagner and Waldteufel, " Die Meistersinger," " The Messiah " and " The Mikado " and Amy Woodforde Finden. But they were entirely deprived of Debussy and Ravel.

At the Ruhleben concert season there were swarms of candidates for the orchestra, and they were not long before they had a Madrigal Society. In the musical season, when the Grand Hall was given up to them every Sunday evening, they had orchestral nights, choral nights and chamber-music nights alternately, and orchestral promenades on Friday afternoon for those who prefered music of a lighter type. On every Sunday morning at ten, as the wit of the magazine expressed it, they had lectures on " the Musik which expresses Humanerty."

In such a milieu the Futurists were not likely to allow themselves to be forgotten. When the magazine brought out its celebrated poster, it pilloried them as talking about its " emotional, psychological, intuitive, prophetic qualities, and describing its evocativity on their self-consciousnesses." It was this poster which raised, quite unintentionally, false hopes among the prisoners by announcing the name of the magazine and its date in this form: " In Ruhleben Camp "—Out To-Morrow.

The Debating Society programmes were of a decidedly cheerier nature. I find allusions in the various numbers of " In Ruhleben Camp " to both a Debating Society and a Talking Club. But the old Ruhlebenites whom I have met do not seem to think that there were two distinct institutions ; one of them suggested that perhaps they called it the Debating Society on nights when they were more formal, and had more serious subjects. The use of the two names in the magazine lends itself to the suggestion, for in the first number the *debates* connected with the expression *Debating Society* were: "That the Metric System be Introduced into Great Britain," which fell through because no speaker could be found to oppose it ; "Plural Voting," and "That Corporal Punishments in Schools should be Abolished." While *the Talking Club*, chronicled immediately below it, had *debates* on "Divorce," "That War is an Essential Factor in the Progress of the Human Race," "That Concentration Camps are an Essentially Retrogressive Feature of Warfare," in which both sides of the house were unanimous, "That Bachelors be Taxed," in which the meeting decided wholeheartedly that bachelorhood was enough of a tax in itself, since they had lived in an enforced state of bachelorhood from the opening of the camp. They also had debates on "War Babies, Should they be Legitimized ? " "Gambling," "Professionalism in Sport," "State Theatres," "Compulsory Elementary Education," "The Degeneracy or not of Modern English Literature," "The

Cinema," " Capital Punishment," " The Success or Un-success of Co-operation in England," " Press *v*. Pulpit," " Woman's Suffrage," etc., showing as time went on a decided tendency to relapse into seriousness—of subject, at any rate.

The most ambitious attempt of the Debating Society was the symposium on " What's Wrong with the World," in which Mr. Pender summed up Mr. G. K. Chesterton's idea of what is wrong with the world, Mr. Rawson summed up Mr. H. G. Wells' ideas on the subject, Mr. Israel Cohen gave an account of Mr. Israel Zangwill's evolution, from the purely objective artist to the political thinker, and Mr. H. M. Andrews dealt with Mr. G. Lowes Dickinson as a political thinker.

The camp magazine said of this last contribution : " This was perhaps the most interesting of all the contributions, because Dickinson was a new name to so many, and it will be the means of introducing one of our most brilliant contemporary writers to them."

Other highly-successful variations were a mock trial, written by Mr. Hamlyn and Mr. Israel Cohen, and a parliamentary election, which Mr.

Cohen described with great gusto in "The Westminster Gazette" of August 8th, 1916. There were Conservative, Liberal and Suffragist candidates, and the last was triumphantly elected at a polling in which two-thirds of the prisoners cast their votes. He had made it clear that he was less concerned about the women's lack of votes than about the camp's lack of women, and declared that if the men wanted their mothers, wives and sweethearts, they should give him their solid support. All the features of an English contested election were carried out in great detail and with great spirit.

These, and later on a Ruhleben Picture-Theatre —in other words, a cinema—were the principal indoor amusements. Card-playing was prohibited at first, but afterwards permitted (on condition that there should be no playing for money), if you took a license out from the captain of your barrack, as if you were a publican or a chauffeur. Loft B, Barrack 2, set the example of pooling parcels of delicacies from home and having tea-parties out of them.

Into outdoor games the prisoners plunged with the national zest of our race. The essentially democratic character of the assemblage interned in Ruhleben Camp was shown by the fact that all other sports paled before Association Football. There was a Ruhleben F.A., and there were even, in the later numbers of the magazine which I saw, football features, such as selection forms for voting about best teams, besides articles by well-known players and reports of every league game (in Ruhleben). There was a ready-made substitute for league-clubs in the shape of the various barracks in the camp, and an elaborate league-competition was started.

Rugby Football was barred at the beginning of the season as being " too rough and not at all a nice game," but eventually a number of international games were played, between teams representing England, Ireland, Wales, Scotland and the Colonies, whose respective successes were as in and out as those of the real International teams in the annual rubber. The Scots-Colonial side beat England and was beaten by Wales ; England beat Wales, and Ireland would probably have won the wooden spoon unless its match against England had been cancelled. That was in 1914.

For the 1915 season the Rugby footballers descended from the Himalayan heights of Internationality to clubs with historic names. Barrack 10, immortal in Ruhleben cricket, called its Rugby Union Football Club "The Barbarians;" Barrack 8 called theirs "Blackheath;" the united Barracks 11 and 5 called their club the "Wasps;" Barrack 3 and the wooden barracks called theirs "The Harlequins;" Barracks 4 and 9 called theirs "The United Services;" and Barracks 7 and 2 theirs "The Nomads."

Cricket enjoys great popularity at Ruhleben, and the various barracks are as keen about securing the championship as the various boarding-houses in our great Public-Schools. But in these house-matches one Barrack, No. 10, so entirely overshadowed the others that not only did it win the championship, but played a combined team of all the other barracks and beat them easily by a hundred and sixty-four runs, L. G. Crosland, who went in first for No. 10, making the astonishing scores of 129 in the first innings and 202 in the second. The scores are doubly astonishing, considering that they were not made on a regular cricket-ground, with a perfect pitch and out-field, and that spiked or nailed boots were not allowed. It was, of course, an entire accident that so many good cricketers found themselves in this particular barrack; there was no system of arrangement as to who should be sent to what barrack, until the German "British" were separated from the rest of the camp and given three barracks of their own.

For golf, of course, proper space was lacking, as the entire sports' ground rented from the proprietors of the Ruhleben Racecourse at fifty pounds for the season was only a stretch of two hundred yards by a hundred and fifty, covering the interior of about half the course. It is extraordinary, under the circumstances, that Ellis should have won the driving competition with a drive of 232 yards.

There were no less than ten well-known golf professionals interned when war began. They were: R. Murray, of Dresden; J. B. Holt, of Hamburg; W. Jackson, of Cologne; E. Warburton, of Kiel; F. Richardson, of Bremen; C. Culling, of Darmstadt; J. Brown, assistant at Berlin; A. Andrews, of Hanover; C. Kyte, assistant at Brussels; R. Cramp, assistant at Hamburg. Murray, who is a North Berwick man, won the championship, after tying with Holt, with a score of 128 for the thirty-six holes.

Lawn-tennis occupies much more space in the magazine. One well-known International player was interned—Mr. G. K. Logie, who lives in Germany and is in the same class with O. Froitzheim, F. W. Rahe, O. Kreutzer and the two Kleinschrots. Another well-known International player in Ruhleben is Mr. J. O'Hara Murray.

Tennis, like cricket and football, had its 'matches between barracks, I presume. It certainly had a tournament, with open and handicap singles and open and handicap doubles, in the last week but one of September, 1915, in which Mr. Logie won the Championship.

Tennis caught on from the beginning, although people are allowed so little money in Ruhleben Camp, and it costs 20 marks to belong to the club, besides the cost of racquets, balls and shoes—at least another 30 marks. People who had money which had been sent them from England lying to their credit with the Captains, were allowed to make purchases therewith, which were approved, at the Camp Stores.

So many people joined from the outset that seven courts could be laid down at once. It was suggested, in a letter to the Camp Magazine, that two of these courts should be set aside for prisoners who were too poor to join the club, but could afford an occasional game if they were allowed to play at a charge of sixpence an hour. The writer estimated that, as three-quarters of the games would be doubles, the club would profit to the extent of seven pounds ten shillings a week.

Another very popular form of sport at Ruhleben was that which is known at Oxford as " Athletics "—meaning running, jumping, and so on. They had an Athletic Sports' Meeting in the Camp on Empire Day. Here, as at golf and tennis and football, there were men with recognized positions in the world of sport. H. Edwards, for instance, ran in the Olympic trials held in Berlin, June, 1914, and was second in the hundred-metre race in the International Sports at Berlin in July, 1914.

The events of the Empire Day meeting consisted of a golf competition for driving and approaching, the former being won with a splendid drive of 232 yards ; a drill-class display ; the 100 yards open ; the two-miles' walking contest ; the 75 yards old age handicap ; the 75 yards open ; the 100 yards jockeys' handicap ; the half-mile open ; the 220 yards open ; the quarter mile open ; the one-mile open ; the 100 yards handicap ; the 120 yards hurdles open ; three-legged race open ; running high jump ; tug-of-war ; relay race, one mile open.

Edwards duly won the four short open races.

The Sports' Meeting produced great enthusiasm, especially the events in which ordinary men were not hopelessly outclassed by the experts. There were very fine entries for the sack and obstacle races, for instance, on the principle, put into words by the editor of the magazine, " I can't run against these nuts, but anyhow, I'll have a shot at something ! "

The other popular sport at Ruhleben was boxing, for which a club with a strong committee was formed, which made its headquarters at an establishment christened " Wonderland," and was controlled by the " Cobbler." The fee fixed for joining the club was very suitable for Ruhleben pockets—one mark—and one of the objects of founding the club was to provide sound tuition at a low charge. Hockey was also played.

I may add, as might have been expected, that there is no surer passport to being influential and respected in the Ruhleben Camp than proficiency in sports.

CHAPTER IX

BEFORE I pay my final homage to the brave men of Ruhleben, I must give the reader the enjoyment of some of its humours, especially those which arose from its trades and advertisements. Not the least amusing of the humours were those which arose from the purely Teutonic Germans who were imprisoned at Ruhleben as British. The real British would not have been unfriendly to them but for the objectionable habit they had of reporting complaints or jibes made against Germany by their fellow-prisoners. As this usually led to seventy-two hours' detention in the cells, where the fare was war-bread and water and the only bed was a plank and the confinement was absolutely solitary, the out-and-out British, called by the

Germans " Stock-Engländer," were uncommonly glad when these people were given barracks to themselves.

The " Stock-Engländer " had regarded with amused tolerance the abuse heaped upon England for having got the German-British into such a hole.

Twice over the whole of the prisoners were lined up outside their barracks, and those who were " Deutschgesinnt "—*i.e.*, those who felt like Germans—and those who were merely " Deutschfreundlich " — *i.e.*, philo - German — were asked to stand out so that their names might be taken.

" We were informed," Mr. Israel Cohen tells us,* " that no practical consequence, either beneficial or otherwise, would result from one's declaration ; but we immediately dismissed this gratuitous monition as a bait, since we could not conceive why the authorities were taking all this trouble if no practical development was contemplated. The general rumour was that the avowed pro-Germans would be favoured with

* In " The Outlook."

frequent furloughs, and even with early release, and this rumour was maintained in spite of all official denials. . . . The holding of such a political Inquisition in a prisoners of war camp seemed to us monstrous. But we soon realized that there was method in German madness. A few days after these preliminary investigations, on a Sunday morning in the middle of April, 1915, the alarm-bell was struck, we lined up in front of our barracks, and we were informed that all the pro-Germans were to be segregated from the rest of the Camp. They were to be lodged in Stable 1, in the wooden barracks 14 and 15, and in the tea-house, which was henceforth called the ' Teehaus.' " Such prisoners in those barracks as were not pro-German had to pack up their belongings and leave their beds behind them, as mentioned in a former chapter, but the pro-Germans were allowed to take their beds with them, as a method of furnishing the wooden barracks, which had only a small supply of beds.

" For over an hour," says Mr. Cohen, " there was a straggling procession in two opposite directions, of prisoners carrying all their goods and chattels—bedding, blankets, books, biscuit-tins, crockery, cutlery, clogs, etc.

" The pro-Germans did not approve of the barracks which had been selected for them, and a good many of them recanted and proudly protested ' Ich bin ein Engländer und bleibe ein Engländer.' Brothers were divided from brothers by the fear of less comfortable quarters, but German-born sons were generally unwilling to remain with their fathers in English barracks for such a reason, though other German-born sons liked the English so much that they refused to accompany their fathers, who had declared themselves pro-Germans for business reasons.

" The English nickname for the P.G.'s was ' Perfect Gentlemen.' "

It was not long before the " Stock-Engländer " discovered—Mr. Cohen's fine article in " The Outlook " of October 28th, 1916, is still my authority—that apart from the loss of their beds incurred by those who had to vacate the Perfect Gentlemen's Barracks, the laugh was all on the side of the Stock-Engländer. Baron Taube, the Acting Commandant, had conceived the idea that the pro-Germans were suffering, or likely to suffer, at the hands of the British in their barracks, as conceivably they might, in some instances, where they had been caught carrying tales against their fellow-prisoners.* It seems to have come to the ears of the German War Office authorities, who decided that either

* In " Germanism from Within," pages 172–173, Mr. A. D. McLaren writes :

" On two occasions all the prisoners were lined up by a genera appel in front of the barracks, and those of German sympathies (*deutschgesinnt*) were called upon to stand out from the rest. On the second occasion (April 18th, 1915) about six hundred stood out, and their names were recorded. Most of the men were either of German descent or born in Germany ; they had become naturalized in England. At no time since the outbreak of the war had I to listen to more virulently anti-British sentiments than those to which these nterned ' British ' subjects gave vent. If I were asked to mention the one thing that made the strongest impression on my mind as the result of my incarceration, it would probably be this fact. The ceremony of renouncing their nationality seems to have been an easy one for Germans in England and our Dominions. Many of those among this element in the camp were virtually spies, one or two of them direct emissaries of the German Government. Over six months ago a prisoner indiscreetly remarked to one of these pro-Germans that he would like to put the Kaiser in the camp for a week and feed him on Ruhleben soup. This was *Majestätsbeleidigung* (*lèse-majesté*) and cost the utterer of the ' seditious ' language several weeks' imprisonment in the Stadtvogtei or Alt Moabit gaol. Since then another Ruhleben prisoner has been charged with this offence. These spies also do good service for their masters in watching for, and denouncing, any prisoners reading an English newspaper, the punishment for which offence is seventy-two hours in the cells."

the pro-Germans must be put into separate barracks, or the Stock-Engländer must be moved to the military camp at Döberitz, a few miles away, which would have been a much greater hardship. So the segregation was an act of kindness to the truly British.

Here comes in the humour. Their fellow-prisoners had all along been wondering why Germans, absolutely pro-German in their sentiments, should have been interned at Ruhleben merely because they were naturalized Englishmen. It now came out. For some reason or other, in this one matter, the Germans felt bound to observe International Law and not compel naturalized Englishmen to serve in the German Army unless they volunteered to do so, and rather than do so the " Perfect Gentlemen " had cheerfully gone to prison. Now it appeared that the authorities, whatever Baron Taube might think, had not given them separate barracks in order to show them favours, but for the opposite reason—chiefly in order that pressure might be brought to bear upon them to make them volunteer.

Mr. Cohen is sardonic about their misfortunes.

Whenever one of them applied for leave, Lieut. Rüdiger, the officer responsible, would ask him, " What regiment would you like to join ? " Fathers were told in so many words that they could secure their own release by the enlistment of their sons. Some fathers prefered to remain in prison rather than send their sons to what they regarded as certain death ; some sons insisted on enlisting so as to free their fathers ; but these unconscripted fathers, when they were freed, led a dog's life and were sent back to Ruhleben for the smallest misdemeanour. One man was brought back for trying to secure compensation from the British Government for his detention at Ruhleben. Others had to remain in the camp because no German town would receive them, being firmly determined not to allow any " Englishman " to live within their domain.

" In other respects," says Mr. Hughes in the " Cornhill Magazine," " the place was like a town, for every man who had a trade could ply it and set up shop. In a few days there were tailors, barbers, bootmakers in practice, and a host of bootblacks, to whom the mud was a friend. . . . Here and there you might see advertisements posted up, as, for instance : ' Young man desires to act as valet to fellow-prisoner for moderate wages ; ' or ' Prisoner will fetch and buy for other prisoners for small commission.' "

The prisoners' magazine, " In Ruhleben Camp," was always enlivened with most humorous advertisements. The advertisers will, I am sure, forgive me for giving them " a free ad." by reprinting their advertisements.

" Why send for Parcels ?—when you can buy all that the heart or the stomach) desires at

" THE BOND STORES.

" Fruit in Season, Tinned Delicacies, Sweets, etc.
Open from 9.30–11 a.m. and 3.30–5 p.m.]
(Sundays closed ; Saturdays open till 6 p.m.)."

" BUTTON can get you anything you want in the sports line. There are some real bargains going in

" CRICKET BATS,
CRICKET SHIRTS,
ETC.

Patronize home industries !
You all know where the shop is.
If you don't, ask a Policeman ! "

" S. SUSSMAN.

Russian Tailor.
Grand Stand No. 1.
(next door to Catholic Chapel).
All work done personally.   Estimates free.
Home address : Barrack 11, Box 26."

" EXPERT COLOURED BARBER.

Also Refreshing Drinks
Lemon Squash.
Between Pond Stores and Barrack 12."

" BOOTS ! BOOTS !! BOOTS !!

(To say nothing of Shoes and Clogs !)
Small repairs done ! Very neat work.
Small patches a speciality.
W. Chapman, Barrack 8, Box 8."

" Try the RUSSIAN BARBER

in Barrack 11.
All the Barrack likes him.
You will like him too."

" SUNNY SMITTY

Some Shoe-Black !
The best in the Camp !
Business hours : 6–10.30.
Black, Brown or White.
Corner Barrack 10."

261

In Ruhleben

"FIRST-CLASS PEDICURE
by
George Teger,
Professional Coiffeur,
Grand Stand."

"THE RUHLEBEN TAILORING DEPARTMENT. Bond Street, W. Gentlemen, we guarantee that all garments made by us are cut and made by the most experienced and practical English cutters, wh› up to internment were employed by the most eminent tailoring firms. Fit, style and workmanship our recommendations.

"Alterations and repairs at our branch between Barracks 3 and 4. Prices under the supervision of the Canteens' Committee.

"We are, Gentlemen, Yours obediently,

"Amalgamated Cutters, Ruhleben."

"Do you want to sell the gramophone?
Or buy an ice-cream machine?
If so, an advertisement in our Exchange and Mart
page will do it for you.
Terms: 1/16 of a page, as per small advertisements
above, M.1.
Special rates for series.
Lost Things Found! Found Things Restored!"

"Clogs ready-nailed. Marks 2.50 a pair tells its own story."

And there were some excellent faked advertisements, such as:

Humours and Realities at Ruhleben

" LONDON YOUTH will exchange strong clasp knife and Football cover for photo of pretty girl. Address, First House, Stall 90, Bar. 1."

" LOST. A Potato. Reward on return to Contractor, Cook House."

" FOR SALE. Return Ticket to London; unused; condition as new. No reasonable offer refused. Address Pessimist, c/o Gatekeeper."

" LOST : Guide to Jerusalem. Finder requested to return same to Homesick, Bar. 6."

" F. J. Davis (Bar. 7). Private Detective Agency. Divorce proceedings a speciality. Missing deck-chairs traced and recovered. For terms apply Green Room, ' Frivolity Theatre.' "

" WE SELL old False Teeth ! Exchange and Mart."

" A SOUL FOR MUSIC. All pianoforte players with a ' fatal ' finger dexterity but without a musical soul should write to Mr. F. Ch. Adler, Care of the Orchestra, Ruhleben, for his magnificent new free book on ' Soul in Music.' "

" STOP ! Don't throw away that old pocket-handkerchief We can make complete sun-bathing costumes from it, as worn on the Spielplatz.

Apply Wyldmann and Co."

263

In Ruhleben

Shopping in Bond Street, Ruhleben, was at first a weariness of the flesh, though afterwards, when it sold multifarious articles, like the one shop which is sometimes to be found next to a Canadian Pacific railway-station at the head of a lonely lake, or a store at a new mining-rush, it became quite a popular institution. At first its accommodation was so incommodious that customers had to form in long theatre queues, and whenever it rained there was a lake in front of it to its very doors.

The Ruhleben Supplies Delivery was called into existence to deal with this. Its advertisement ran :

" RUHLEBEN SUPPLIES DELIVERY

" Will collect orders for canteen supplies between the hours of 8–9 a.m. and 1.30–2.30 p.m. and will deliver morning orders before mid-day and afternoon orders before 5.30. Orders collected by representative wearing a red band. Tariff : 5 per cent. to be charged extra for delivery, cash with order or deposit accounts. Inquiries to the Ruhleben Supplies Delivery, c/o office of this paper.

> " No more waiting in the line for an hour.
> No more long queues in the cold and rain.
> No more breaking engagements.
> No more worry—give your order.
> Pay and we do the rest."

There was also a Ruhleben Express Delivery, like our messenger-boy system in London, which advertised that it would undertake all branches of regular post-office service, such as forwarding parcels from one person to another, within the camp, registered letters, special express letters, and so on. Its advertisement ran :

" RUHLEBEN CAMP EXPRESS DELIVERY. Letters or post-cards sent all over the camp. Stamps can be bought from the messengers. Post in boxes fixed to barracks and at all important points of the camp. Why waste time in rushing round the camp to look for your friends ? Drop a note in the R.X.D. letter-boxes. It will only cost you 1/3d."

It entered very much into the life of the camp ; it is constantly cropping up in the magazine.

Little by little the Ruhleben Camp Stores made good. When the canteen was started in 1914, in the words of its advertisement, " you could only buy trousers and marmalade, and perhaps half a dozen other articles " there. But when once the Camp Authorities had hit upon the idea that you might not buy from an outside source anything which was sold at the

Camp Stores, the Camp Stores naturally began to forge ahead. Camp shops, says the advertisement, do not, must not push new goods; nothing is kept in stock except what the public has demanded.

Sometimes the camp has to be reminded, " (1) That we are in a concentration camp; (2) That it is war-time, and that prices are fluctuating from time to time as a consequence; (3) That we are in Germany, and that such things as English tobacco are not to be had just outside the gate."

The Camp Stores have ten departments. Each has a manager responsible for stock-taking and cash accounts. At the Food Canteen stock is taken daily; at the Dry Goods Store fortnightly. New supplies are handed in at the Stores' Office, where they are checked and an order handed out to the Military Authorities. On receipt of new goods stock is taken and compared with the invoices. In fixing prices only running expenses are taken into consideration; the Stores' " Committee " fixes them. The stores are not run at a profit, but at a considerable loss. If any department makes a profit, it is applied to the reduction of food prices; in the Food Canteen most articles are sold below cost; other departments generally make five per cent. The way in which such losses are covered was explained in the Finance Committee's report:

"The amount of M.29,091.81 appearing in the Surplus Profits, etc., Account represents the total derived from donations, library fines, proceeds of concerts up to the formation of the Entertainments' Committee, and profits arising from canteens, dry stores, boiler-house, etc., from November 6th, 1914, to June 30th, 1915."

The stores do not have to pay the cost of running themselves any more than the other institutions of the camp do. The British Government supplies the money for this, through the American Embassy. It was therefore decided to apply the surplus to reducing the selling price of the most essential articles of food, such as butter, eggs, vegetables, etc., which are much cheaper inside the camp than they are out.

"It is no light task," says the writer, "to

cater for a clientèle of 4,000, and it must be remembered that all our shop-keepers are absolute amateurs. It is interesting to note some of the figures for the week ending August 31st, 1915, in no way an exceptional one, by the way. During the eight days 2,102 lbs. of butter, 815 lbs. of margarine, 805 lbs. of cheese, 162 lbs. of sausage, 418 lbs. of ham, 2,300 tins of condensed milk, 3,286 lbs. of sugar, 25,138 eggs, 119 lbs. of bacon and 120 lbs. of salt."

Alas ! it is much easier now, for neither butter, eggs, bacon, canned milk, canned meat (or any other kind of meat)—hardly any necessaries of life, in fact, have been on sale in the canteen since the beginning of 1916.

The opinion of the camp magazine about the stores is worth quoting :

" What makes life in Ruhleben bearable ? How many would give a correct answer ? Many would say, our manifold interests, such as sports, theatricals, or education ; others would reply, that it is only the advent of the morning and evening papers, giving us a shadowy idea of the great events progressing outside ; while yet another group would assure us, that it is only the hope and everlasting expectancy of release that keeps them from the brink of a nervous collapse.

" Upon sitting down and thinking the matter over, however, there seems only one reply which will apply to all sections of the camp, viz., *Bond Street.*"

The Dry Goods Store has a hundred and forty-three different kinds of articles in stock, and presents a very different spectacle from the long queues in the snow which used to be formed for English tobacco in the times in which it was an exciting day when English marmalade came in. In the Dry Goods Store the best-selling article is a species of electric-battery, of which eight hundred were sold in a week. The runner-up was Sunlight Soap, of which five hundred bars a week are sold; *Sunlight* is one of the things which are subsidized and sold at a loss. Five hundred note-books sold in a week; that points to a burning thirst for improving the mind. There is what the magazine called " a generous output " of Brilliantine and a turnover of a thousand sheets of brown paper a week. As brown paper plays no seeming part in education, this puzzled the buyers for the Ruhleben Stores, until they remembered that brown paper and drawing-pins are the greatest assets for comfort and privacy in a barrack loft. In the early days of Bond Street sufficient knives, forks and plates were sold to fit out four camps. Insect powder gradually fell off, but the demand for frying-pans was ever increasing.

There is a Special Order Department. Articles not in stock must be ordered through it. Orders made in private or business letters are returned by the Military Censors to the Stores Office. Personally I cannot help wondering if the paternal German authorities have an interest in the Stores; it is usual for German authorities to be interested.

Beds and mattresses are not kept in stock; they are considered too bulky, though the largest business done in the Dry Goods Department is in them. All kinds of decorations for boxes are in great demand.

This accounts for the flamboyant advertisements of a certain Mr. Josephson. In the third

number of the magazine his advertisement
asked :

> " Why does everybody rush to the Ruhleben Carpentering Works—
> First Shed in Rear Barrack 7, opposite Barrack 5—to consult Mr.
> Josephson ?
> " Because he knows how to make their Ruhleben lodgings cosy,
> comfortable and healthy.
> " Because Mr. Josephson, who is a London builder, with 25 years'
> experience, knows how to do it.
> " We are not cheap-jacks—but we are prompt and reasonable."

And in the eighth number he returns to the
charge with :

> " Ah ah !   This is the Ruhleben Carpenter.
> Mr. Josephson, opposite Barrack 5.
> He knows how to make Ruhleben lodgings cosy,
> comfortable and healthy.
> Is your chair broken ?
> Do you need a bedstead ?
> Or any other repairs ?
> Go to him at once."

One of the humours of the Stores was the sale
of shilling suits of summer clothing, ordered by
the American Embassy for prisoners who were in
need of assistance. The shilling did not represent the value of the suit; it was to prevent

anyone from asking for a suit who did not require it. Otherwise it would have interfered with the interests of I. Steinbock, the Ruhleben tailor, in the Grand Stand Hall, who advertised suits from 40 marks, summer suits from 20 marks, trousers from 12 marks, white linen ditto from 5 marks.

The report of the American Ambassador showed that the shilling summer suits were a great success.

When anybody wanted anything, he asked the Captains to write to the American Ambassador about it. It is to be presumed that the Ambassador's clerical staff gave him some assistance in dealing with his Ruhleben correspondence, even though it was " official " from the Captains. The magazine mentions a certain " Reggie," like the dear, delightful *Reginald* of " Saqui," who wanted his relations to understand that it was better that they should send him presents of articles which did not signify if they were sent in duplicate, such as bottles of liqueur from Morel's, because he had all the George V. prayer-books and large paper editions of the Omar Khayyám which he needed. This " Reggie " is represented as pestering the Captains to write to the American Ambassador to say that he wants baccy and grub, not underclothes, his relations having asked the American Ambassador to see that he wrote at once if he had not enough thick undervests. And anyhow, how was he to write to his best girl if the people at home wanted a postcard every week ?

The magazine also quotes a gentleman who wrote to the Ambassador that as he had only expected to be away from home for five days, he had left his false teeth behind. He had been at Ruhleben five months, he said, and the meat was getting lumpy. Would the Ambassador send to England for his teeth. This seems to have been an actual application, because it is recorded that he was provided with a new set in the camp.

Then there was the question, according to the magazine, of the interpretation of the limitation " for personal use." One man wished to order a hundredweight of cigars and half a ton of cigarettes, solely for personal use, and the Captains discovered that he was a non-smoker. Another gentleman ordered fifty pounds of coffee

273   18

and twenty-five pounds of sweets, also solely for personal consumption.

Another humour mentioned was the question of parcels, on which the Captains—of course with the British Government Funds supplied through the American Ambassador—had to pay various charges when they arrived, and then find out whom they belonged-to, the parcels including every kind of unreasonable articles, from ladies' wigs to Otto-Sauer grammars. Telegrams and telephones were also an embarrassing feature. The Captains used to be asked to send them and wait for payment until remittances arrived from England.

The Camp Library was started on November 14th, 1914, with 83 books, received from the American Ambassador and Mr. Trinks. In addition, books were received from the Seamen's Mission at Hamburg and Mudie's Library, etc. By July, 1915, they had 2,000 English books, 2,000 English and American magazines, 300 German books, 130 French books. On the average, 250 books a day were taken out. They even decided to print a catalogue; the camp had a printer.

The kitchen inspectors resigned because they were expected " to make turnips taste like aspic jelly and transform a lump of common or garden porker into *pâté de foie gras*." They were evidently not men of the same calibre as Col. Sir Edward Ward, Bt., K.C.B., who when he was in Ladysmith, converted the starving horses into a beef-tea paste called *chevril*, which seemed as good as Bovril to the hungry Ladysmithies. One wonders that its name has not been perpetuated in commerce.

Among the other chief camp institutions were church services, a police-force, and fatigue-parties. The fatigue-parties were not in the nature of whist-drives or progressive euchre, but were a force of paid volunteers, paid with the money of the British Government, to do the cleaning-up and other hard work of the camp.

This work was at first done by calling for workers from each barrack in turn, until it was found impossible to obtain any workers from some of the barracks, which are not mentioned, but may be taken to be the barracks where the Perfect Gentlemen resided, so that the work all fell on those barracks which were amenable to *noblesse oblige*. Even at these barracks which did all the work a large number of men deliberately disappeared as soon as volunteers were called for, so that the bulk of the work was done by practically the same men on every occasion.

The fatigue-parties were always in charge of a soldier and generally required in a hurry. Owing to the difficulty of securing men, the soldier in charge frequently completed his gang by commandeering any passer-by, irrespective of age or suitability for the work to be done. The system of commandeering anyone caused great dissatisfaction in the whole camp, and continual friction between the prisoners and the authorities. Moreover, the work done was extremely inefficient.

Next, they divided all the men fit for work in each barrack into gangs of fifteen men with a foreman, who were to be called upon in rotation. Any member of any gang had a right to provide a substitute and, if necessary, to pay him a fixed fee.

The scheme broke down immediately. The gang whose turn it was to do the work disappeared and volunteers had to be called for again.

During all this time a very strong conviction had been growing in the camp that interned civilian prisoners could not be compelled to work, accordingly many men, when they were called upon to work by the authorities, flatly refused to do so. Sometimes they were reported; sometimes no notice was taken; but in either case they were not punished.

At last came a time when many tons of potatoes and other foodstuffs of the camp arrived at the Ruhleben railway-siding, and the prisoners were ordered to provide gangs of men to unload the trucks and haul the contents in carts to the far end of the camp, half a mile away. Most of the men commandeered were totally unaccustomed to manual labour and the work proceeded so slowly, and the friction between the prisoners and the authorities became so acute that it became absolutely necessary to make a change in the system.

After much discussion it was decided that the only permanent solution was the establishment of paid working-gangs. This method was adopted at once, and has worked excellently ever since. The system of payment being recognized, other necessary workers were paid out of the British Government money, supplied through the American Embassy. The wages paid for the kitchens, which cooked for 4,000 men and employed 76 to 78 men, amounted to 464 marks (£23 odd) weekly. The German authorities had reckoned that they ought to cost £7 10s. weekly, all told—surely the most economical management on record, as it would have meant wages of under 2s. each per week, even when the four chefs were thrown into the averages ? So they paid £7 10s. and the British Government rather less than £16.

The chefs and the butchers received 12s. a week each ; the foreman potato-peelers, the boiler-men, the wagon-men and the firemen 6s. a week each ; the washermen 6s. or 7s. a week each ; washermen-helpers and stores-carriers 6s. each ; a miscellaneous helper 3s. and a stores assistant 8s. The six prisoners who kept the Lazaret clean received 5s. each ; the four men who carried food from the kitchens to the Lazaret 3s. each ; three of the attendants at the *Schonungsbaracke* (or Convalescent Barrack) received 5s. each and one 3s. weekly. The seven bathing attendants, who attended on 600 men daily for hot shower-baths, in addition to pumping water into the boilers, heating the boilers and keeping the establishment clean, received 1s. a day each. In the office the typist got 5s. a week; two of the messenger-boys 2s. 6d. each and one 2s. The man who looked after the schoolrooms for the Education Department received 5s. a week and the post-office cleaner 1s. a week. The attendant at the wash-house (there was only one) received 5s. a week.* One carpenter received 7s. a week and the other four 5s. each. The special fatigue-parties drawn from Barracks 14 and 15 received from £1 to £1 5s. a week between them. The lavatories were cleaned and disinfected by one foreman at 10s. weekly and five men, who received 7s. a week each. The drains were kept in order by two men who got 3s. 6d. a week each and the fire-brigade had only two paid men, who got 2s. a week each for looking after the hose-pipe and sprinkling the yard when dusty. The

* As time went on various laundries were started in the camp, including a Japanese laundry.

total money spent upon the fatigue-parties came to about £17 a week. The wages all told cost the British Government about £44 5s. a week—not much over £1 per hundred prisoners.

The foreman of the fatigue-parties received 10s. a week, without overtime; the men 5s. a week and overtime at proportionate rates. The hours of working are 8.30 to 11.30 a.m. and 1.30 to 4.30 p.m. On Saturdays they only work in the mornings.

The principal occupations of the fatigue-parties were to empty the rubbish-bins placed in front of each barrack; to haul the stores, such as potatoes, rice and sugar, from the railway-siding, 150 yards outside the camp gate; to construct paths with the ashes from various engineering works, through the desolate morasses which stretched from end to end of the camp; to relay the drains from the kitchens and lay fresh drains from the lavatories; to drain the parts of the camp which continued morasses; and to perform gardeners' work in a small wood outside the boundaries of the camp, which was reserved for the use of the officers of the garrison.

The fatigue-parties included, in October, 1915, 4 foremen, 34 cartmen, 10 roadmakers and 15 sundries. The prisoners had their own police force and their own fire-brigade, who were, like the post-officials, barrack-cashiers, sub-captains, librarians, kitchen-inspectors, etc., unpaid.

The bathing-facilities were so extended that anyone who did not have a bath at least once a week was punished by the German authorities as well as by public opinion. There was also a boiler for supplying hot water at about ½d. and eventually for ¼d. a can, the proceeds being applied to reducing the prices of food. But the laundry-facilities were not on a par. There was no special laundry provided ; the wash-houses or sheds had to serve for the purpose. There was no hot water, of course, and no drying accommodation anywhere. In the winter, the drying was done in the boxes, lofts and wooden sheds where people sleep.*

The greatest grievance of Ruhleben all through seems to have been the want of large, well-

* As time went on some of the prisoners started in business as aundrymen ; various advertisements of laundries are to be found in the camp magazine.

lighted and well-warmed rooms, during the long months when people are compelled to be indoors, to accommodate the various classes of the alfresco university by day, and people who wished to have somewhere where they could sit about and smoke and talk without paying any entrance-fee at night.

Mr. Gerard, the American Ambassador, writing on November 1st, 1915, said:

"A properly heated and lighted recreation and assembling room is certainly extremely desirable for the damp and cold winter-time. A new barrack has been sanctioned by the military authorities for the purpose, and I will do my best to press the work. I might venture to suggest that if so many private individuals had not occupied necessary space by erection of private clubs, the military authorities would be more willing to grant permission for the erection of further buildings intended for public good. Further, if the very men, such as the 'Camp Committee' (who were all members of the 'Summer-house' Club), had devoted some of the energies which they expended upon the erection of the club for their own private use to the construction of a public sitting-room, the building might already be in use."

I suppose that in reality it all came back to the same reason which here in England prevented us from having armaments that the Army and Navy had over and over again pronounced necessary—viz., getting the Treasury to provide the money. Probably if Mr. Gerard had asked permission for the building to be erected with British Government money, it would have been done at once, since the German authorities showed no objection to various British clubs erecting premises for themselves. The clubs made sure that they had the money before they asked for permission. Of course, if they had been willing to spend their funds on paying for the recreation room of the camp, instead of asking the German authorities to provide it, it might, as Mr. Gerard says, have been provided much sooner. Probably, also, they did not see why they should, although the Camp Committee may all of them have been members of the Summer-house Club. There is the yet further probability that some of these clubs may have been started because their members had no liking

283

for the classes and entertainments so popular with the majority.

I had almost forgotten the church services, to which I began to allude above. Ruhleben was well off for them. They had Church of England services every Sunday, with the British Chaplain from Berlin in charge on the first and third Sundays (and the fifth Sunday, whenever there was one, I presume), and with the Hamburg Seamen's Mission in charge on the second and fourth; they had a Communion service on the first Sunday; also a Wednesday Evening Service of a broad and undenominational character, which seems to have been suspended during the summer, and a five minutes' Evensong held in the open air, on the Third Grand Stand, every evening at nine, which could only have been in the summer: a quarter to nine was bedtime in the winter.

Roman Catholics had a Solemn Mass, with Sermon and Benediction at 8 a.m., in the Grand Stand Hall on Sundays, and Mass every morning at 6.30 a.m. in the chapel; and they had Rosary and Benediction on Sundays and Thursdays at 7.30 p.m.; and Vespers on Sundays at 4 p.m.

The priest, Father Schmidt, of Cambridge, Cape Province, S.A., lived in the camp voluntarily.

There was a German Protestant service from time to time, conducted by a Moravian preacher from Berlin, and attended presumably by the " Perfect Gentlemen."

When the United States Ambassador prepared his last report to His Majesty's Government, there was no Y.M.C.A. hut in the camp,* but the American Y.M.C.A. had plans for a new hall, costing probably over 6,000 marks, about to be commenced, with six class-rooms for the special use of the Education Committee, and a share of the use of the hall for lectures and classes.

The Church Army has taken a very considerable part in sending parcels to the prisoners who have no friends of their own to send them. There were, when the last report was issued, sixteen hundred British subjects drawing relief funds. No one would have fared worse than the

* In the letter dated January 16th, 1916, it will be seen that a Y.M.C.A. hall (American or English) had been built and was in full working order.

three hundred German "British," whose official name is *Heimatslose* (countryless men), if it had not been for the instrumentality and largely for the personal generosity of Prince Max of Baden, who raised a large relief fund, large enough to send a weekly package to a hundred of these men, containing a pound of jam, three-quarters of a pound of sugar, half a pound of sausage, three-quarters of a pound of condensed milk, a quarter of a pound of cocoa ; or a package containing a tenth of a pound of sardines, three-quarters of a pound of condensed milk, three-quarters of a pound of sugar, eighty grammes of soap and a quarter of a pound of cocoa. Was it fair—this alternative of sausage or soap ?

The two most ordinary types of British relief packages were : (1) One packet of biscuits, one tin of tongue, one quarter-packet of tea, one-half-tin of milk, one tin of golden syrup, one tin of potted meat, half-pound tin of margarine, half-tin of cheese. (2) One packet of biscuits, one tin of compressed beef, one half-pound tin of margarine, one pound-tin of cocoa and milk, one tin of golden syrup, one tin of sardines, one half-tin of milk, one tablet of soap. Here the alternative was between soap and cheese—which suggests other comparisons.

The Hon. Secretary for the Distribution of Relief in Kind at Ruhleben said that there were about two hundred and fifty men in the camp who did not receive parcels from any source, and that their requirements would be best met by parcels containing : tins, half a pound of margarine and one pound each of milk, meat and jam ; packets, half a pound of sugar and a quarter of a pound of tea. The large deliveries of bread from Switzerland, shipped by the Société de Guerre, paid for in England and addressed to individuals, declined from 5,560 four-pound parcels in April to 4,930 parcels in May, because the quality had become so bad. It arrived very dried-up and extremely hard, and on mastication became gummy and stringy. There were 800 bad packages in April, and considerably over 2,000 in May.

The bread from England, which is in transit from two to five weeks, suffered from mould. The two English breads which always arrive in perfect condition are those of John Barker and Co. and the Army and Navy Stores.

In Ruhleben

While I was talking about Church services, I forgot to quote the eloquent appeal of the Church of England to the camp, published in the camp magazine :

" The CHURCH in the CAMP.

" IN ENGLAND the Church has had a wonderful awakening in the last ten months.

IN RUHLEBEN the Church needs fuller support to help to spread the same awakening spirit.

" IN ENGLAND there has been a great revival of Family Prayers ; the late Lord Roberts started the movement.

' IN RUHLEBEN there is five minutes of common prayer every evening at nine o'clock.

" IN ENGLAND the churches have subscribed thousands of pounds for the sufferers in the War.

" IN RUHLEBEN there are no collections at the services ; we only ask you to come and give them your support.

" If you cannot take part in the Church of England Services, come to the Wednesday Evening Service, which is popular and free in character, but

" Do come to one of them !

" The Camp Services are got up by men in the camp FOR the camp, and suggestions and advice are always welcome."

Last of all I come to the question of punishment and release. The punishments, said a returned Ruhlebenite, were petty and contemptible. Anyone found reading an English paper (and a copy of "The Times," whose introduction cost a sovereign, did get into the camp every day), or smoking inside barracks, or wandering about the camp at night, was liable to seventy-two hours in the cells, on a diet of dry bread and cold water.

Also there were punishments for things said in letters. One man was taken away from Ruhleben altogether for writing, after the first French offensive, " I think that things are looking serious for the Germans."

One of the worst instances was that of the Captain of one of the barracks, who was summoned before Baron Taube, the Acting Commandant of the Camp, to explain why a certain little group of Englishmen had been laughing. The Captain explained that they were not laughing at the soldiers at all, but at something else, and satisfied the Baron that this was so. At the same time the Baron said, " Well, you must have respect for us, we are Germans." The Captain said, quite respectfully, " Yes, and I am an Englishman," and was sentenced to twenty-four hours in the cells for it.

Since the granting of Home Rule at Ruhleben,

which was in September, 1915, the prisoners have had much more freedom inside the barracks, since the soldiers were withdrawn from them altogether and the preservation of order left entirely to the representatives of the prisoners themselves. The police-force selected from them were given a new police-station about the same time, but it is chiefly used as a lost-property office.

The parcels post office was naturally one of the chief institutions of the camp, because it distributed about a thousand parcels daily among the four thousand prisoners—and on one occasion, at any rate, as many as sixteen hundred.

About fifteen hundred prisoners applied for release on the ground that they were unfit for military service. Slips could be obtained from the captain of each barrack on which a prisoner could state why he considered himself eligible for release to England as militarily unfit, and they naturally were very keen to do it.

Very different to them was the young New Zealander who said to my returned Ruhlebenite, a few days before he left, "Well, I have one brother in the trenches, and if I could get out of this I'd very soon be by his side ! "

There were many of his kidney in the camp. One of them, quoted by Mr. Hughes in " The Cornhill Magazine," said to an American lady who was permitted to visit the place and speak to the prisoners, when she asked him if he was content with his food and lodging, ignoring her question, " Madam, whatever you write, don't write that we blame England for this. The Germans say they will let us go if the English Government release the prisoners over there ; and the Government won't, and we are content. We will not be released, if it would be awkward for the War Office at home." And that, says Mr. Hughes, was the common sentiment of the camp.

In one of the magazines there was a delightful little poem on this great subject of release :

" THIS YEAR, NEXT YEAR—

" This year, next year, now or never ;
    That's the question—shall we ever
See the spuds and onions growing
    In the cabbage-patch at home ?
Watch the kiddies gaily blowing
    Bubbles from the soapy foam ?

In Ruhleben

" Sitting by the fireside fender
　Roasting chestnuts on the ember—
(Sweet the memory, and tender)—
　You and wifey—you remember.
This year, next year, now or never ;
　That's it—damn it !—Shall we ever ? "

And with this we may take leave of Ruhleben.

THE END

Printed at The Chapel River Press, Kingston, Surrey.